W9-CEW-327

Other Travelers' Tales Books

COUNTRY AND REGIONAL GUIDES

*America, Brazil, France, India, Italy, Japan, Mexico, Nepal, Spain,
Thailand; Grand Canyon, Hawai'i, Hong Kong, Paris, and San Francisco*

WOMEN'S TRAVEL

*A Woman's World, Women in the Wild, A Mother's World,
Safety and Security for Women Who Travel,
Gutsy Women, Gutsy Mamas*

BODY & SOUL

*The Road Within, Love & Romance, Food,
The Fearless Diner, The Gift of Travel*

SPECIAL INTEREST

*Danger!, There's No Toilet Paper on the Road Less Traveled, The Penny
Pincher's Passport to Luxury Travel, A Dog's World, Family Travel*

FOOTSTEPS

Kite Strings of the Southern Cross

FOOTSTEPS: THE SOUL OF TRAVEL

An imprint of Travelers' Tales, the Footsteps series joins a grand tradition
of travel writing, unveiling new works by first-time authors, established
writers, and reprints of works whose time has come…again. Each book
provides a story that will fire your imagination and feed your soul.

THE SWORD
OF HEAVEN

THE SWORD
OF HEAVEN

A Five Continent Odyssey to Save the World

Written and Photographed by
Mikkel Aaland

TRAVELERS' TALES

SAN FRANCISCO

The Sword of Heaven: A Five Continent Odyssey to Save the World
By Mikkel Aaland

Copyright © 1999 Mikkel Aaland. All rights reserved.

Travelers' Tales and *Travelers' Tales Guides* are trademarks of Travelers' Tales, Inc.,
330 Townsend Street, Suite 208, San Francisco, California 94107. *www.travelerstales.com.*

Credits and copyright notices are given starting on page 260.

Jacket and Interior Design: Diana Howard
Cover photographs: Water copyright © 1999 by Masano Kawana/Photonica.
   Kami copyright © 1999 by Mikkel Aaland.
Interior Photographs: Mikkel Aaland
Page Layout: Cynthia Lamb, using the font Bembo

Library of Congress Cataloging-in-Publication Data
Aaland, Mikkel, 1952-
   The Sword of Heaven: a five continent odyssey to save the world/written and with
   photographs by Mikkel Aaland
   p. cm.
   ISBN 1-885211-44-9
   1. Peace—Religious aspects—Shinto. 2. Aaland, Mikkel, 1952- 3. Shinto—Social
   aspects, I. Title
BL2220.3 b.A35 1999
299'.56117873–dc21   99-38755
                                                           CIP

First Printing
Printed in the United States of America
10 9 8 7 6 5 4 3 2 1

For my daughter, Miranda Kristina:
May your enlightened heart guide you.
And to my wife, Rebecca:
I love you.

It is not power that corrupts,
but fear.

Aung San Suu Kyi
Winner of
the 1991 Nobel Peace Prize

prologue

The Amazon.

It was my last Shinto god. I was aboard the *Marreiro II,* a weathered jungle boat, as it struggled against the merging currents of the Rio Negro and the Rio Solimoes just outside the Brazilian town of Manaus.

This god, like the one I had placed two weeks earlier in South Africa, and the one I had placed a week earlier near the place where Brazil, Argentina, and Paraguay meet, and all the others, was wrapped in white prayer cloth and imprinted with ancient Japanese symbols: *ten* (heaven) and *ken* (sword). I leaned carefully over the wooden railing, weak from a fever that had gripped me the day after I placed the god at the Cape of Good Hope. It grew worse as I spent days in the jungle searching for the proper resting place for the last god in my possession.

Below me were the Rio Negro, full of minerals and humus and as dark as a bat's cave, and the Rio Solimoes, full of light Andean silt. They mixed like oil and water. I looked up from the primordial gumbo, through the moist air, only to see where huge patches of the verdant jungle had been ripped from the earth to make room for factories made of concrete.

This place is an ecological mess, I thought. I was mindful both of Shinto's worship of nature and aware that most of the jungle-destroying factories were Japanese-owned. It's not perfect, but nothing ever is.

I removed the white cloth to uncover another familiar barrier, this one of plain white paper. Just before the boat burst free from the mottled mess and entered the Negro, I heaved the heavy stone overboard. Just as the circles in the water faded, a pink dolphin, which the natives call "devil fish," swam by. The boat's only other passenger, a high school biology teacher from New York, cried out in sheer joy at the sight of the exotic mammal. He began clicking his camera madly.

I felt better the instant the hollowed stone, filled with its precious contents, splashed into the water. I watched with tears in my eyes as its impact blended the brown and black stew, creating a third distinct color, one richer and more beautiful. The mixed water, now called the mighty Amazon, moved leisurely downstream toward the distant sea.

Nearly six years had passed since I had first heard of the Sword of Heaven. Six years, five continents, and several trips to Japan. What started as a peace project to save the world had quickly become much more, shaking the core of my Western beliefs and bringing long-forgotten demons to the surface. Now, with this last god placed, my part in a grueling and marvelous project was over. Perhaps, I thought, tonight I can finally sleep in peace.

PART ONE

*When
the spring gushes forth,
it does not know at first
where it will go.*

chapter 1

My first placing in Norway.

In the early fall of 1982, the relative calm of the '70s was over, and the Cold War was back in full swing. The Soviets had invaded Afghanistan and placed deadly SS-20 missiles on the border between the USSR and Western Europe. Under the leadership of President Ronald Reagan, the United States responded with new and more potent weapon delivery systems such as the Trident submarine, the B-1 bomber, and Peacekeeper missiles. Tens of thousands of nuclear missiles were ready to launch. All it would take would be a small spark to ignite the atomic flame that would destroy the world.

At a dinner party in San Francisco, the conversation turned from adventurous tales of the Orient to the apocalypse. After all, in those days, it was a dangerous world. Sometime during our frightful discussion, one of the dinner guests—Juan Li, whom I would come to know well—told us a remarkable story he had heard while traveling in Asia.

"Shinto is Japan's indigenous religion," he began.

Most of us nodded yes. I had heard that Shinto was similar to American Indian spirituality, focusing on nature and ancestors.

"Many years ago," Juan continued, "shortly after the bombing of Hiroshima and Nagaski, a Shinto priest had a horrific vision of the end of the world. His spirit was crushed. He became despondent."

Juan paused for a moment, tugged on his scraggly moustache, and carefully watched our reaction with soft yet intense eyes before continuing.

"But then the priest had another vision, a vision of how to save the world. He was inspired."

The priest was instructed by God to break an ancient Shinto relic—the Sword of Heaven—into 108 pieces and then encase each piece in stone. The stones—which now were considered *kamis*, or gods—would take on special powers and become capable of battling the evil that engulfed the world.

Juan explained that, a Shintoist, like the priest, believes that evil results when nature and one's ancestors are not properly worshipped. Shintoists also believe that gods or spirits dwell inside inanimate objects. A stone, a sword, a jewel, a rainbow—anything that evokes or inspires awe or the divine—can possess power and become a *kami*. And like the ancient Greeks, the Shintoists have a pantheon of gods to whom they pray.

Followers of the priest, Juan told us, began to place the stones in a protective ring around the world. After each stone was placed, special ceremonies were held during which the priest and his followers left their physical bodies and joined the heavenly gods in the ensuing battle. But the battle was going slowly: at this time only a few of the 108 stone gods had been placed.

"Who told you all this?" someone asked.

"One of the teacher's disciples, a young Japanese man named Kazz Tagami," Juan replied.

Juan's answer satisfied the questioner, but I still had doubts. Stone gods? Out-of-body travel? I liked Juan, and I wanted to believe him, but this was the stuff of fiction, not fact.

"How do you know the story is true?" I asked.

"Well, I just placed a god," he answered matter-of-factly. "In Taiwan."

With this revelation of his involvement, my curiosity increased. Could a Shinto priest really save the world? Could a Shinto priest save us from an unthinkable nuclear catastrophe?

Like most of the others in the room, I grew up in the '50s

and '60s with the bomb and the Cold War as a constant back-drop. In addition, my father was a scientist at the Livermore Radiation Laboratory, which in the 1950s became the United States' major nuclear weapons research facility. Because of the Lab, we knew our town was marked with giant **X** on Soviet strategic maps. My Livermore classmates and I accepted the idea of nuclear annihilation the same way that other generations accepted plagues, famine, and economic calamity. There was nothing we could do, and yet we had little confidence in the so-called nuclear priests—the politicians, scientists, and military leaders—who were in charge.

The idea that a lone man with magical powers in a far off land could affect this situation seemed far-fetched. Nonetheless, through the years of accumulated despair, a faint hope stirred in my heart. What if his powers were real?

As the evening ended and guests said their good-byes, something compelled me to give Juan my address and to offer my help, even though I really didn't expect anything to come of it.

"A package arrived for you." My father looked troubled. As the train slowly departed behind us, I shouldered my camera equipment and luggage to his car. "It caused a lot of confusion at customs: they wanted to hold it."

"What are you talking about?" I asked wearily. After finishing magazine assignments in West Germany and Czechoslovakia, I was headed to the family home in southern Norway. My father had recently retired from his job in California and was spending part of the year in the house he was born in.

"News travels fast here," he said in heavily accented English as he squeezed his large frame into the car. "People are already talking."

As he put the key in the ignition, he wiped his head, thinly covered with strands of white hair.

"Here," my father finally said, handing me the customs declaration. "What does this mean, 'One Shinto God'?" I quickly took the packing label from his outstretched hand.

"Where is the package? Did they hold it?"

Starting the car, he turned to me and said, "They didn't open it. It won't get us in trouble, will it?"

I had no reason to believe that the package contained anything dangerous or illegal, but how could I be sure? My response was tinged with more than a little false confidence.

"Of course, it won't get us in trouble."

"Good," he said. "It was heavy so I left it at home."

We drove in silence for a while. The single-lane road, eight kilometers long, wound through forests of evergreens toward the town of Ulefoss and the family house. Occasionally the forests were broken by freshly harvested fields and the traditional red farmsteads of Telemark.

The road widened as we entered the outskirts of town. On our left, a wide river paralleled the road, and except for a family of wild swans, the river was undisturbed. Across the river was dense forest.

Between the road and the river were widely spaced homes. Each plot of land has a name. We passed Odden, which means "Rock Jutting Out into the Water"; Deilevja, "Dividing Inlet"; and Baerland, "Berry Land." Finally we came to Aaland, "Land by the Water," a piece of land near a small creek and a river. Like many other rural Norwegians, my grandfather had taken his surname from the name of the land where he was born. My father, born on the same land, also chose the name Aaland.

We crossed the creek and slipped through a narrow opening between my grandfather's store—where he had made and sold furniture—and the house. As the wheels of the car hit the gravel, they sprayed tiny pebbles into the small courtyard behind the house.

My father turned off the engine and sighed. He stared across the river for a minute to the forest on the far side.

"How're you enjoying retirement?" I asked, my eyes following his to the forest.

"You mean 'forced retirement,'" he grunted. His accent was less pronounced as his thoughts abruptly shifted back to America. "Kristian Aaland. Successful scientist. Fired. I feel so useless. This wouldn't have happened here in Norway. Thirty years of service. Here they have laws. Here they show respect."

"You saw it coming," I said gently. "The Lab gave you plenty of signs."

His downward slide had begun ten years earlier, after I left home for college. The Lab had moved to replace older employees like my father with younger, lower-paid scientists. But after nearly twenty years as an electrical engineer, my father's grip on his only security in America was so tight that he dug his heels in deep and resisted. Ten years later, he was finally forced out, bitter and disillusioned.

Dad turned to me and spoke sharply. "And you? Flying here and there. Living month-to-month. No wife, no kids. How can you understand what I did?"

He saw the pained look on my face. We had argued about this too many times before. I was 30 years old and between girlfriends. I'd published two books, and managed to make a decent living for ten years selling photographs and articles to magazines in the United States and Europe. I knew he was proud of my survival in a difficult profession, but I also knew that he thought of me as his idealistic oldest child, one who didn't show enough concern for money and other earthly things. Of course, I thought he showed too much concern for those same material things.

"I don't know what you are waiting for, son," he said.

There was a long silence.

"Have you heard from mom?" I finally asked, groping for some neutral ground. Mom was in Livermore, teaching emotionally handicapped children in the public schools system. She was born in Wisconsin and grew up in the U.S., and although she loved Norway, she only accompanied my father to his homeland occasionally, during summer breaks.

"She called this morning. Everything is fine."

A small fishing boat glided swiftly downstream.

"This sure isn't Livermore!" I exclaimed, marveling as I always did at the difference between my ancestral home and the tightly placed, nearly identical suburban houses of my California hometown.

"No, it's not Livermore," he said, suddenly impatient with our conversation.

"My restless father," I thought, as he reached for the car door. He rarely sat still for anything or anyone. I glanced to my left and noticed without much surprise that he had begun rebuilding Grandfather's workshop, a barnlike structure near the water, full of tools and machinery used to make furniture. He'd also started remodeling my Grandfather's furniture store, an adjacent structure that ran long and narrow from the river to the road.

He hadn't changed. In Livermore, he had altered our tract home into something so unique that townspeople would drive out of their way to see it. The garage was turned into a workshop; the kitchen, the living room, and dining room were remodeled; and a towering three-story addition, crowned with a sauna, was added in the backyard. Tired of us kids damaging the trees, my father had also made a metal tree by welding together large iron pipes of different widths.

Metal roots kept the towering structure from falling, even when my two younger brothers and I and six neighborhood pals hung from it.

And then there was the bomb shelter. He built it in 1962, shortly after the Berlin Wall was erected, the same year as the Cuban missile crisis, and the year we thought the world would end. He'd wanted to build one before, but when President Kennedy publicly suggested that private bomb shelters were good for the country, it became much easier for my father to get the required permits and financing. My father bought half of a Southern Pacific boxcar from a railroad junkyard, disassembled it, and transported it to our front yard. For the next six months, night after night, he welded it together. When he was finished, he hired a crane and an operator to tear up our front lawn and dig a hole 30 feet deep. He then had the same crane lift the assembled boxcar and drop it into the hole. Finally, the whole thing was entombed in concrete.

The shelter was finished in October, just in time for the Cuban crisis. At first the entire family—my parents, my two brothers, and I—slept there, but after a few weeks, when the crisis subsided, everyone else returned upstairs to the house. I remained, and the bomb shelter became my bedroom until I left home for college, eight years later.

"You want to see the package, the Shinto object?" my father asked, peering back at me through the open car window. "Go to your room, unpack, and I'll bring it to you."

In the tiny guest room, I stacked my luggage in a corner.
I noticed my father's high school graduation picture hung on
the wall. In the picture, he looks just like me: slender with
long, straight, blond hair, and a high forehead. He gazes out
from behind the round eyeglasses that were popular in the
30s and 40s.

Through the open window, I heard him closing a door,
then shuffling across the gravel toward the house. "He'll want
answers," I thought. "What am I going to tell him?" Then I
remembered the letter.

It had arrived two weeks earlier, while I was photographing Germans in a bar for a magazine article. It was
sent to me care of my friend Wolfgang and was written in
clear, legible handwriting—but in an English so awkward
that I had to read everything twice. Now, I pulled it out of
my suitcase to refresh my memory.

"I am a friend of Juan Li," it began.

"He gave the letter that you have a interest to put god. I
know that everything prepares by God, even in each our
meeting. I am very glad that God bless you by your interest
in this putting. The story of the putting is very long, I will
explain you someday...."

The writer ended his letter by asking whether he should
send the god to West Germany or to Norway. It was simply
signed "Kazz."

I had written back, acknowledging receipt, saying that the
"god" should be sent to Norway.

As my father entered the room, I put the letter away, still not sure what to say.

The "god" was in his hands. It was packaged in cardboard, which was covered with Japanese symbols. As I reached for it I noticed that it cost 6,000 yen—more than $30—to send by airmail. I tore the cardboard away. Inside, a bricklike object was wrapped in white cloth imprinted with more symbols. There was a letter, but I folded it and put it down next to me.

"Well?" My father stepped back into the doorway. I lifted the god up and down. It weighed as much as a small barbell. What part of the curious story would he believe? I'd never even heard him use the word "God" before. I placed the god on the floor.

What did Juan tell me about the project? I took a deep breath, struggling to remember details.

"Be patient," I told my father. "I know this will all sound strange to you."

He leaned heavily against the door, clearly not patient at all. I spoke quickly, first describing the dinner party, then the Shinto priest's doomsday vision, then his "instructions from God," and finally the priest's act of breaking the Sword of Heaven into 108 pieces and encasing the pieces in stone. I told my father the little I knew about Shinto, and when I was finished I picked up the god.

"And that is a piece of the sword?" my father asked.

"Seems so."

"Go on," my father said.

"That's all, at least all I can remember."

"But who sent you the package?"

"A man named Kazz. I don't know much about him either. He is a friend of Juan, the guy at the dinner party who told the story and got me involved."

"And what do you know about Juan?" my father asked.

"Not much," I confessed. "He travels a lot. He's very knowledgeable about the Orient. I think he sells antiques for a living. But I'm not really sure. I just met him."

"So we have a story you heard from someone you briefly met, who heard it from someone else?"

"Yes," I said, a bit sheepishly.

My father was silent. Then he asked, "And this priest. Who is he? He went to all this trouble because of a nightmare?"

Now it was my turn to be silent.

"And this group, the followers of the teacher, who are they?"

"I don't know. I just thought it was a great story. I didn't know it would come to this," I said, pointing to the god.

My father's face was impassive. His look reminded me of when I was fifteen years old, trying to explain American football to him, which I played but he never watched. I trailed off; he nodded and left without a word. Leave it alone, I thought, it's too late. His world has always been one of logic and rational thought, not of spirits or gods or football.

I picked up the heavy object, lay back down on the bed and found the letter that had come with it. It was brief, just like the previous one. It said that I should not take the god into the bathroom because that was considered "unclean," and that I should place it where I wanted, but preferably in water, the source of life. Again, the letter was signed simply "Kazz."

The god sat in my bedroom for a week while I helped my father repair the leaky workshop roof and prepare the house for winter. We worked together in the strained, compromised fashion of fathers and sons. I found fault with the way that he did things, and he found fault with all that I did.

One morning I went to chop wood, wondering why he insisted on so much wood, and found that my ax was covered with frost. Every day the sky grew grayer and colder. Then, one morning at breakfast a week after I arrived, it began to snow. The long, dark Nordic winter had arrived. As my father watched the flakes stick briefly to the kitchen window, he said, "Time to go back to California."

After his matter-of-fact proclamation, he went back to reading the morning paper. I saw the headline and reached across the table and pulled the paper from him. The story was about massive peace demonstrations in West Germany, with

100,000 people in Bonn marching against the proliferation of tactical nuclear weapons. I figured my friend Wolfgang was there.

"A neighbor asked about the Shinto object," my father said suddenly. "The guy at the post office must have talked. I told her your story. What are you going to do with it?"

I dropped the paper.

We had ignored the topic since his initial grilling, and I figured that he had dismissed the entire thing as another wild fantasy of an idealistic son.

I told him I was thinking of taking the god back with me to West Germany.

"Use your head," he said. "What about customs?"

Of course, he was right. As I passed through foreign customs, "God" in a heavy cardboard box might look a bit suspicious. I could show the inspectors that the parcel was not full of drugs or explosives, but I'd still have to spend time explaining what would surely sound like a crazy story.

"What do you think, Dad? What should I do?"

"You know the lake where your great aunt owns a cabin? It's surrounded by a national forest, and fed by an underground spring. Since Shinto worships nature, put it there."

He pushed away from the table, stood up, pulled his wool cap over his ears, and with a determined stride headed to the door, leaving me surprised that he had shown some interest in my story after all.

A few days later I hiked with my father out from the small town up to the lake. The snow had been replaced by a light drizzle that made the green pine needles glisten like jewels. Our steps released pungent odors of moss and dried grass. A few birds dove for cover as we passed.

I stopped while he yanked on a tangle of vines growing in the path. Tossing them to one side, he moved on. I waited a moment.

"Dad," I said, catching up with him, "There's more to the story. I didn't tell you everything."

"Now what?"

"When Juan Li told me the story, he mentioned some odd things. In Taiwan, just as he was placing a god in a lake, a furious storm stopped, as if by magic. He told me he saw a photograph of a god with a strange glow surrounding the case. This may not be as simple as tossing a stone in the lake...."

"Son...." my father interrupted.

"Not that I believe it...." I fell behind him again.

We came to a narrow path that led to my great aunt's small wooden cabin. The rustic structure was perched on a huge slab of granite jutting deep into the middle of the lake. My father checked to see that the windows, boarded up for the winter, were secure. As he did, the sun broke through the clouds. The granite under his feet sparkled.

I walked to the edge of the granite where it abruptly

dropped six feet into the lake. Motionless water perfectly reflected the surrounding trees. I unwrapped the white cloth from the stone. My father insisted on taking a photograph of me and the stone god. I protested, but only briefly.

I pulled back my arm, then heaved the stone god high in the air, over the granite, past the shore, and into the lake. It made a splash no different than a common stone; concentric waves of water rushed toward shore. The water that shot up in the air seemed to explode like fireworks. As each ring came toward me, the mirror image of the trees was disturbed, making the water look like an Impressionist painting.

I took pictures until the first wave hit the shore, thinking that Kazz and his group would appreciate this record of the placing of their god.

When my father asked me what I would do next, I really didn't know what he meant.

"After Germany, you mean?" I asked.

"No, I mean with the Shinto thing."

"That was it," I said. "They only sent one. I'm finished. Maybe I'll write a story about it."

He nodded.

On the way back into town my father's step seemed lighter. He was more talkative.

"Those Vikings, your ancestors," he said, "they also believed spirits dwelled in nature. They were connected to the earth. They also respected the elders and tradition...."

His voice trailed off. We passed through the rest of the forest in a comfortable silence.

That evening a group of curious boys gathered on our porch. Somehow the story that the Shinto god had been placed in the lake had spread rapidly through the town. I hadn't told anyone; it must have been my father. They asked questions: Where exactly had we thrown the object? Were we sure it was stone and not gold? I told them what I knew about the Shinto priest's vision and his struggle for peace. The young Norwegians listened intently.

As they left, I followed them to the road and heard them talking with great excitement. A few were already making plans to dive for the object come summer when one of them, the smallest, protested. "But just think," he said, "if war comes we'll all be protected. We must leave it."

I went back to tell my father what they had said, but he was already asleep.

chapter 2

Shinto gods arrive at my home
in San Francisco.

*In 1983, a group of scientists including the noted astronomer Carl
Sagan proposed the nuclear winter theory, which hypothesized that
the smoke from the fires following a nuclear war would darken the
skies for months, interrupting the normal flow of life on earth and
wiping out the human race. Groups such as the Physicians for
Social Responsibility, led by the Australian-born pediatrician Helen
Caldicott, and the Union for Concerned Scientists, were tireless in
bringing the message that winning any nuclear war was impossible
because the earth would be so contaminated that survivors of a
nuclear war would envy the dead. They used photographs of
victims from Hiroshima and Nagasaki as proof that little could be
done in the face of radiation poisoning. The massive antinuclear
weapons demonstrations occurring in Europe now exploded in
American cities such as Boston, New York, and San Francisco.*

After I returned to California from Norway, I wrote to Japan and sent Kazz the pictures of the placement of the god. He replied that the lake was a fine place, and thanked me for the prints. The project was going slowly, he wrote; only 34 of the gods had been placed, and the world situation continued to worsen.

I tracked down our mutual friend, Juan Li, and told him about the placing in the lake.

"Perfect," he said, without surprise.

Encouraged, I told Juan of my plans to write a story for a local newspaper about the project. Even though I still doubted that throwing a stone in a lake would make the world safe, I had good feelings about the project. It had brought me closer to my skeptical, rational father, even if just for a few moments, and had reminded him of a world of connections and respect he had not found in America. It had also given at least one scared Norwegian boy the confidence that people from a faraway land were concerned about peace. I wanted to share my positive experience with others.

"Maybe the story will generate some support for the project," I explained.

"Good idea," Juan Li replied. He was moving from San Francisco to Toronto—he was always, it seems, traveling somewhere—but he promised to stay in touch.

The writing of the newspaper article came easily. I described the priest's vision of a "network of peaceful energy" and the afternoon with my father at the lake in Norway. I mentioned Kazz, Juan's mysterious friend, who had become my link with the priest and his other followers. I sold the article to the *San Francisco Examiner*'s Sunday magazine, *California Living*. With its circulation of more than one million, I figured someone would read the article and offer to help Kazz and his teacher.

My part in the project was done.

The newspaper article appeared three months later, on a beautiful spring day, which made the storm that it created all the more strange. On May 16, 1983, I went biking in Golden Gate Park, forgetting that the article was scheduled for publication. Several hours later, I pedaled back to my house, a turn-of-the-century Victorian that I shared with two roommates. The light on my answering machine was blinking, madly signaling at least a dozen calls. As I dragged my bike into the basement, I wondered what was going on. I didn't usually get calls on Sunday.

Before I could play the messages, the phone rang. It was a friend from Palo Alto, who wanted to tell me that he was at a picnic where people were talking about my article. Most thought the project was a great idea, but one older man had come apart. He had been stationed at Pearl Harbor, and all he could remember were the kamikazes—winds of god—barreling from the sky.

"This guy said the Japanese pilots were wacko, totally insane," my friend recounted. "And he said their passion came from their devotion to the emperor and to Shinto. He said connecting Shinto with peace was a joke."

After we hung up, I played back my messages. They were all from friends who had seen the article, which ran as a double-paged spread with two of my photographs. Most just wondered if there was anything they could do to help, but there were a few skeptical comments, and those were the ones that stuck in my mind.

I returned one phone call to a friend who asked me jokingly, "How do you know there are only 108 stone gods?" He suggested that the Japanese were producing gods like Toyotas or Minoltas. When I admitted that I had no proof or corroboration for the story, my friend—who had lived in Tokyo—said, "The Japanese are masters at keeping things vague. They do it purposely so they can fit things to meet their own needs." He didn't say it directly, but he implied that you couldn't trust them.

Another friend reminded me on the phone that the practice of Shinto was outlawed in this country during World War II. If a Shinto shrine or other object of worship was found at places like Manzanar, a detention center for Japanese and Japanese-Americans in remote southeastern California, punishment by United States government officials immediately followed. In San Francisco, a Shinto shrine was torn down at the Japanese Tea Garden in Golden Gate Park. "As far as I know," he said, "it's the only time the practice of a particular religion has ever been outlawed in the United States."

A friend of a friend was offended by the implied object worship and totemism, and cited the biblical account of Moses and the golden calf: *Do not make idols or set up an image or a sacred stone for yourselves, and do not place a carved stone in your land to bow down before it. I am the Lord your God.* "Thousands of years of progress, and you talk about worshipping stone gods!" she said. "What about the other pagan practices, like human sacrifice? What do you think of that?"

My friends weren't the only ones reacting. On Thursday an *Examiner* secretary called. "What should I do with this batch of mail?" she asked. "I've never seen so many letters in response to an article." Some came from as far away as Oregon and Alaska.

Unlike some of the frank comments from friends and acquaintances, the letters were all positive. No one brought up kamikazes, emperor worship, or totemism, or blamed Japan for yet another global conspiracy. An American Indian from a Cheyenne tribe in western Oklahoma noted the similarities between Shinto and his beliefs, and wrote: "The way of my people is to respect the earth, placing the good of the whole group before yourself...although we have different names for our gods, I believe we are all one people who pray for, work toward, the same goal—peace."

One letter was from a man who had a private sanctuary, a spring, in his backyard where he offered to place a god. Another was from a person who, because he practiced yoga and was a vegetarian, felt he had the prerequisites to help. One woman was so desperate to get in touch with Kazz and his group that she had called directory assistance in Japan trying to find his number.

The offers of help were nice. But I found myself feeling oddly irritated just the same. Isn't it a little desperate, calling directory assistance? And isn't it a bit selfish, wanting to put a god in your own backyard? Did they think my article was an ad in the personal section? An offer to write in and get a spiritual fix?

Finally, I made copies of all the letters offering help. I put the originals in a large envelope and mailed them to Kazz. No reason, I decided, to grow possessive of something that wasn't even mine. I was sure Kazz would be happy to see all the offers of help.

He was not.

Seven days after I sent Kazz the package, I received a letter from him. It was most direct. "I am very surprised at the writing because I thought our work is not open to the public."

Not open to the public? Juan Li had encouraged me to write the article. In my first letter to Kazz, I had told him that I made my living publishing stories and photographs. What did he think I'd do?

The worst was to come.

Kazz began talking about bad spirits, who were after me. "Because of this writing in the newspaper, you are," he said, "one window for the world and the first target for bad spirits."

He ended the letter with words that seemed to taunt me. "You have to keep your mind all the time. The man who has a connection with God project has a great responsibility."

What the hell did Kazz mean when he wrote I was a target? Did he actually believe that there were entities that would swoop out of the sky like kamikazes and blast me? Or formless spirits that would maliciously create havoc in my life? Were they the same spirits he believed were engulfing the earth and causing all the problems?

I tossed the letter angrily onto my desk. In all my years of writing and photographing for magazines, I'd never been threatened with bad spirits.

I'm not superstitious. Bad spirits are merely a manifestation of some inner conflict or need. They are a psychological phenomena, an illusion of the mind. They are therefore explainable rationally. This is Kazz's problem.

Anyway, as long as I didn't believe in them they couldn't hurt me, could they?

During the next few weeks, letters crisscrossed the Pacific. Kazz was trying to figure me out. "I asked my teacher about your writing in the paper, and he asked God. God told him that this is one part of the next new spiritual wave. You should explain everything."

I wrote and apologized to Kazz and his teacher for the breach of confidence. Kazz replied: "There is no problem. We know that we are one member of great project. Each one has a special individuality, and because we came from the God world to this human world, we are all the body of the God of Universe."

"All in the same boat," I muttered to myself, translating Kazz's strange choice of words into something familiar. "I shouldn't get so caught up in this bad spirit thing. I can figure it all out later."

Then, just when it seemed that Kazz and I were beginning to understand (or at least accommodate) each other, there was a loud thud at my front door. I was having lunch with a friend, but I got up from the table and ran to investigate. The door was open and sitting inside the porch, bathed in afternoon light, was a large package. No one was around.

"The Body of Shinto God Five Peaces Cased in Stone Box," read the customs declaration. The package weighed 8.8 kilograms.

Gods on my porch?

A baby would have been less confusing.

Kazz didn't send any instructions where the gods should be placed or to whom they should be given. Then, on the very next day, a similar package arrived, this time under the arm of a disgruntled postman who complained profusely about the weight. Inside were five more gods.

Sending a god to me in Norway had seemed an act of faith—a statement about Kazz and Juan Li's friendship. Sending me ten more seemed crazy. I hadn't even met this man, yet he was sending me ten of his sacred gods.

What had I gotten myself into?

chapter 3

Me circa 1964 inside the bomb shelter.

*In March 1983, in a move seemingly meant to diffuse the enormous
public outcry and fear over nuclear escalation, the president of the
United States announced a plan to "protect" the country with a
network of laser weapons and killer satellites that would sit just
outside the earth's atmosphere. This umbrella would, in theory,
render enemy missiles useless and therefore discourage attack.*

*The major responsibility for developing the so-called "Star
Wars" technology went to the Lawrence Livermore National
Laboratory, formerly the Livermore Radiation Laboratory, my
father's former employer.*

*On June 20, 1983, more than 950 people were arrested for
demonstrating outside the Lab. They carried signs that read,
"Livermore, City of Death." There was widespread belief among
the demonstrators that Star Wars was an offensive move that
would accelerate the arms race.*

Three days after the arrests I drove to Livermore.

In front of me, at the end of East Avenue, was the Livermore Lab. Next to me, inside my gym bag, was a Shinto god, the first of the ten that Kazz had sent to me several weeks before.

I wiped sweat from my forehead, keeping one hand steady on the wheel. It felt wonderfully hot. Just a 55-minute drive away, in San Francisco, it was depressingly cold and foggy.

I planned to stop briefly at my parents' home, pick up the family pass to the Lab recreation center, one of the only perks my father had been allowed to keep, and then head to the Lab pool.

The Shinto god?

I hadn't forgotten Kazz's threat of bad spirits, and I was still confused by many of the responses to the newspaper article. But the Lab, a nuclear weapons research center, seemed a perfect place for a Shinto god.

After all, there were Hiroshima and Nagasaki to consider and I had ten gods to get rid of.

My mother met me on her porch. She was holding a newspaper with a picture of a demonstrator being dragged away by the police.

"They are so angry," she said, clearly upset that Livermore was receiving such notoriety.

I gave her a kiss on the cheek and then glanced quickly at the photograph. "Mostly scared," I suggested.

I walked toward the living room but remained standing. I was in a hurry.

"You want lunch?" my mother asked as she passed me on her way to the kitchen.

"No thanks, I should be going. I really crave some sun."

She walked into the living room and sat wearily on the couch. My father was back in Norway after spending the winter in California. My mother would join him in a few weeks.

"Sit and talk, please," she said.

"Next time, I promise."

I shifted from one foot to the next nervously.

"On the radio," she said looking up at me, "someone called the Lab 'Auschwitz West.' Can you imagine?"

That comment stopped me and I stared at her incredulously. I thought, damn the Lab. Not only had it made us a top priority for Soviet nuclear missiles, but now, because of this ridiculous Star Wars plan, it was making my hometown the ridicule of the peace-loving world.

"You sure you don't want lunch?" my mother said when I didn't respond.

I just shook my head.

"Well at least do me a favor. Check out your old room, would you?"

As she spoke, she reached for the pool pass that was sitting on the fireplace mantel and then handed it to me.

"With all the rain, I'm afraid your room flooded. Your father got most everything of value out before he left. Maybe you want to salvage something. It'll only take a minute."

"Sure, sure," I said, annoyed that time spent checking out the flooded old bomb shelter would cut into the time I'd planned to spend in the sun.

"And take a flashlight!" my mother called out as I headed toward the long hallway and the concrete stairs that led down to my bedroom. "Your father turned off the electricity."

Technically, it wasn't a bomb shelter, since it wouldn't have survived a direct hit from a thermonuclear device, but rather it was a radiation shelter. It also wasn't a claustrophobic capsule like the bomb shelters advertised in the magazines of the time. My father never worked in small scale. The Southern Pacific boxcar, which provided the basic frame for the shelter, was plenty big enough for the entire family. However, no one in the family liked it quite like I did. It was warm in the winter, cool in the summer, and always quiet. And I was safe, which was important because I didn't want to die in a nuclear holocaust.

There were seventeen concrete steps, just as I remembered from childhood. The last few were underwater. As I

waded into the cold, knee-deep water, my flashlight illuminated an old photographic enlarger, rusted.

No use trying to save that, I thought. I hadn't used it since
high school, anyway. Can't believe I actually made pictures
with that archaic piece of junk.

I turned the light to the concrete walls, then to a solid
metal hatch, which I had painted fluorescent orange in the
late 1960s.

I knew that beyond the hatch was a metal pipe, three feet
in diameter that angled 45 degrees to the surface. It was a
combination escape hatch and air vent. On the opposite end
of the shelter another similar pipe shot straight up to the
surface at a 90-degree angle. When the shelter was first built
the pipe continued, past the surface, ten feet into the air. This
way, when you escaped, you could avoid stepping in the
radioactive fallout that had accumulated on the ground.
Since it blocked the view from the front window of our
house, my father eventually tore the pipe down and sealed it
off at the surface.

Next to the angled, bolted hatch was my old metal cot.

The flashlight died. I shook it and it revived. One more
sweep of the room—a file cabinet, empty; shelves that were
once full of canned foods. Now there was only the Geiger
counter. I reached for the familiar instrument, but the
batteries were long defunct. I placed it back on the bare shelf.

There was nothing I wanted so I turned back to the stairs.

I didn't notice the wind on my neck until I was nearly on the stairs. Although it was warm and faint and smelled of summer trees, it affected me like a blast of icy Arctic air. My head snapped back. My body froze as if someone· were holding a gun to me. I knew that the air must be coming from the escape hatch, which had never been sealed properly, but even with this rational explanation I panicked.

Then I stumbled, and the darkness swallowed the flashlight, which fell out of my hand, and old childhood demons rushed to surround me.

Suddenly Kazz's warning leapt to my mind. "You are now the first target of bad spirits."

I sloshed madly through the water, smashed into a concrete wall, groped my way around it, and then dashed up the stairs. I bid my mother a hasty, breathless goodbye and left for the Lab.

A few blocks from my family's house is East Avenue, the main artery that connects the Lab with the town. I drove past Callahan's mortuary and the cemetery. In my rear view mirror I saw the tall stucco tower of Livermore High, from which I graduated in 1970. On my right was the East Avenue Elementary School, which I attended from kindergarten through the eighth grade. I passed churches, grocery stores, and, farther out of town, the vineyards that provide grapes for Wente Brothers, one of Livermore's two wineries. Except for the flat-roofed buildings at the end of East Avenue, it was a typical suburban scene.

I parked in the recreation center's visitors lot. It was almost empty, and there were no demonstrators. I walked quickly, the Shinto god lying in my gym bag next to my swimsuit and towel.

These buildings and the Lab were built in 1952, the year I was born. A few years earlier the Soviets had exploded a nuclear bomb, and in response the United States Department of Energy was given a virtual blank check to expand America's nuclear capabilities. Scientists from all over the U.S., and even other countries, poured into Livermore, where tract homes went up as rapidly as the flimsy shacks of California's gold rush days. A sleepy town known for its rodeo, wineries, and railroad station changed quickly into a modern town of science. A sign on the outskirts of town read: Livermore, the Atomic City.

The Olympic-sized pool was in the center of the giant complex, but it was surrounded by a fence that kept it as a separate island. A single fenced walkway led from the parking lot to the pool, flanked by guard towers that made sure no one wandered off the path.

I lay on the grass near the pool, surrounded by children of Lab employees. Even with a slight breeze it was hot. I swam a few laps, then went back to the grass, reveling in how serene I felt.

Slowly, the afternoon sun dropped behind a guard tower; the long shadows of buildings fell across the grass. The lifeguard's whistle sounded. I sat on the grass and watched people leave the pool.

I took the Shinto god from the bag.

Suddenly I didn't feel all that well.

I paced around the perimeter of the pool like a nervous animal, near the fence and bushes. There wasn't really any reason why I couldn't have simply found a hidden spot under some bushes and dug a hole for the god. None of the guards could see. And if they did, so what? I was merely planting a stone, nothing dangerous, nothing threatening.

But there was no denying it. Something was very wrong. In the depths of my consciousness, I could sense the faint stirrings of something struggling to surface.

Something to do with the Lab, my childhood…something to do with the panic I felt earlier in the bomb shelter.

I tried in vain to find the connection, but the harder I tried the more elusive the something became. What was it? I felt a barrier that kept me from remembering, a wall stronger and more fortified than the one physically surrounding the pool and the Lab. What was on the other side? I didn't know. I only knew that for all practical purposes I was paralyzed, unable to perform the simple task of placing the Shinto god.

I never did place the god at the Lab.

Instead, as that summer day in 1983 ended, I grabbed my towel, the god, and as my father had done for 30 years, joined the other stragglers from the pool and the throngs of scientists dressed in white shirts and ties as they filed out the gate to drive home.

chapter 4

Juan Li at a restaurant in San Francisco's
Mission District.

*In a survey of the high-school class of 1979, 50 percent of the
sample reported that advances in nuclear weaponry affected their
thoughts about marriage and the future, and a majority said they
were even affected in their daily thoughts and feelings. There were
vivid expressions of terror and powerlessness, grim images of nuclear
destruction, doubts about whether they will ever have a chance to
grow up and an accompanying attitude of 'live for now.'"*

—*Baby Boomers* by Paul C. Light

Juan Li picked another serendipitous time to enter my life,
calling me two weeks after my afternoon at the Lab pool. We
met at a small Chinese restaurant near my house in San
Francisco's Mission District. He told me that he had read my
newspaper article and liked it.

"But," I said sternly, "you should have warned me that Kazz considers the Sword of Heaven a secret project. I would never have written about it had I known."

"Sometimes I can't figure Kazz out," Juan replied. "He never told me it was secret."

"Well, it's not now," I said nervously. I described the responses I had received to the article, both the positive and the skeptical.

"And to be honest," I continued, "I'm having some second thoughts."

His big eyes were bright, amused by what he saw as my naïveté. "There is nothing simple about Shinto or the Japanese."

"I know," I said softly.

Juan was silent. I told him about the strange arrival of ten more gods. He looked surprised. "Did you ask for more?"

"No," I said. "Do you want them?"

"At the end of the summer, when I go back to Canada, I'll take one," he said. "But I'll be traveling until then. Why not give them to some of the people who offered to help?"

"I will. But some of them seemed so desperate."

He stared at me intently. "Then why don't you place another one?"

I gulped my Coke and ignored his question, choosing not to tell him of my aborted try at the Lab. Instead, I told him that one of Kazz's letters had threatened me with bad spirits.

"Bad spirits?" asked Juan leaning closer to me.

"Those were his words."

"Kazz is superstitious," he said. "He sees bad spirits every-where. But whatever you call it, any action releases forces in response."

"Action like trying to save the earth…"

"*Any* positive action will meet negative resistance."

"You don't think bad spirits are a psychological phe-nomena?"

"Psychological?"

"In the head."

Juan looked thoughtful. "That's a very Western concept, the idea that the mind is separate from the world. In Shinto, and other Eastern religions, there is no distinction."

"So you believe in bad spirits too."

"I didn't say that. I just said that resistance is a natural ebb to life's flow."

Juan grinned at my frustrated look.

"Because of the newspaper article, Kazz said I was the first target. Why target me? "

"I am sure he didn't mean only you. He meant anyone who helped. After I placed a god in Taiwan, at the Sun & Moon Lake, a cloud opened up and a beautiful ray of light lit a huge pagoda on the shore. I told you that already. But that night I had a dream, and I knew that by my action I had exposed myself to something very dangerous. By writing the article in the newspaper you've just made yourself a bigger target."

"Wonderful. And it's not even my project."

Juan pulled back in his seat. "Are you sure?"

After a long pause, I said, "Maybe you better tell me more about Kazz." I was more eager than ever to hang flesh on the man behind the strange letters. "Who is this guy? Exactly how did you meet him?"

For a moment it looked as if he wouldn't answer my question. Then he asked: "What have I told you?"

"Not enough." My irritation was showing.

"It was really an amazing coincidence. I met Kazz in Kashmir in 1976."

Juan had arrived by bus in Srinagar, Kashmir's capital. It was evening, and he was quickly hustled for a place to stay. Someone insisted he stay at a houseboat on the lake, where another Japanese "like him," was staying.

"My mother is Cuban, my father is Chinese," he explained. "For some reason, in India, I'm always confused with the Japanese."

I looked at his face, a handsome blend of Eastern and Western genes, and understood.

The Japanese boatmate was Kazz. He had already been there a few days, waiting for a storm to subside before continuing on his way.

"In truth, though," Juan said, "Kazz was a bit of a lost soul. He wasn't sure what he was doing or where he was going."

As travelers far from home, Juan and Kazz quickly learned much about each other. They both loved books and antiques.

When Kazz learned that Juan had studied Tibetan Buddhism for twelve years, he wanted to know more.

"But it is a very difficult religion to describe," Juan said. "I still find it confusing. Then I remembered Bon, the pre-Buddhist belief of the Tibetans. It's very similar to Shinto."

Bon worshipers, Juan explained, believed in a cult of divine kingship, much like a Shintoist worships the emperor. They also believed gods lived in the air, the earth, and the underworld. As with Shinto, Bon's powerful essence— the belief in a unifying spirit world—was passed by song and dance from generation to generation, rather than by written text. This essence was eventually absorbed by the Tibetan Buddhists.

"I assumed Kazz knew about Shinto," Juan continued after he told me about Bon. "He didn't."

"But he's Japanese," I said.

Juan shrugged. "He associated Shinto with World War II and militarism, and didn't want anything to do with it."

They spent a few days on the houseboat together before Kazz decided to accompany Juan to Ladakh, a desolate mountainous region, home for many of the Tibetan people. In 1974, after decades of isolation, Ladakh's Indian rulers finally began allowing foreigners to enter.

Juan and Kazz spent a month together, visiting monasteries on the high plateaus and seeing sights that no outsider had experienced in modern times. During their travels, they continued sharing stories and even swapped acquired skills. Kazz showed Juan how to make prints by rubbing rice paper on rock and wood. Juan, who had turned his knowledge of antiques into a profitable business, showed Kazz many of his own tricks—how to detect fakes and how to avoid trouble at borders and customs. By the time they parted—Kazz to Japan, Juan to Nepal—a great friendship had formed.

They stayed in touch by mail. In 1978, two years after they met, Kazz returned to Nepal and they met up again.

"He was still wandering, still searching," Juan remembered.

"No Shinto, eh?" I said.

"Not yet."

Given their shared interests, it was inevitable that, on a purely practical level, Juan and Kazz would collaborate in the antique business. That meant that Juan would eventually travel to Japan.

"Kazz didn't have a phone, and I arrived at his home unannounced," Juan remembered. "He was getting married the next day. He never told me! But he made me his best man. Part of my responsibility was to sing a traditional song—in Japanese—but I sang it in Spanish instead."

After the wedding, Kazz told Juan about a Shinto teacher with whom he had begun to study.

"What changed his mind about Shinto?" I asked.

"I don't know. Maybe it was the teacher. Maybe he got tired of searching. You'll have to ask him."

My thoughts turned to the 5,000 miles of ocean that

separated me from Kazz, and I wondered if I would ever get the chance to ask him myself. Then Juan added, "The important thing is that Kazz was no longer a lost soul."

"Did you meet the teacher?"

"Yes. He was very interesting. And a very powerful man."

"Tell me more about him."

"More?" Juan smiled. "You'll have to meet him yourself."

"Okay, you liked him. Kazz liked him. Then what?"

"The teacher and his disciples had already started the project placing the gods. They began in Japan, but they didn't have much experience with the outside world. Kazz, with his years of searching, could travel with the efficiency of a pilgrim. He offered to help. He was perfect for the project, and the project was perfect for him."

"When was the last time you saw Kazz," I asked.

"More than two years ago, in 1981, here in San Francisco. He had placed gods in India, New York, Peru, and even the Antarctic. He was here to place another one."

Juan stopped as if to remember. Then he shook his head. "What a day!"

Kazz had arranged for a skipper and a sailboat to take him beyond the Golden Gate Bridge to the Pacific Ocean.

"I went along." Juan said. "The bay was calm, but just past the bridge the water was dark and violent. We nearly capsized...."

"When was this?" I asked, a little too intensely.

Juan Li looked surprised by my question.

"In 1981."

I grasped his arm. "No, exactly."

He thought a moment. "The first weekend in March." He looked down at my grip. "Why?"

"Go on. Never mind. What happened to Kazz?"

Juan looked at me a long moment before continuing.

"Just after Kazz threw the god overboard, a huge wave struck the yacht. Kazz was thrown against the railing. He was badly hurt, but he didn't tell me until he was back in Japan a few weeks later. He wrote and told me that his back hurt so much he couldn't travel."

Juan saw my distant gaze. "Are you listening?"

"Sure." But I wasn't really. I was stuck on a remarkable similarity between Juan's description of the near disastrous voyage and an experience of my own—on that same first weekend of March 1981, a year and a half before I heard of the Sword of Heaven.

I had just finished a photography assignment in Chico, a small town in Northern California. My client suggested that we visit Madam Ruby, a fortune teller who lived within walking distance. "She's very good," my client said when I showed reluctance.

Ruby greeted us in the waiting room and motioned for me to follow her. When we were alone in a separate, smaller room, the robust lady gently picked up my hand. She talked about my two brothers, and seemed to know that they are younger than I am. She said my father was having a hard time, and I replied that he was being forced into retirement. And yet, even though she was telling me things about myself and my life that required intimate knowledge, I remained the skeptical son of a scientist. Still, I pressed on, asking her about my future.

She held my hand firmly. "You are so impatient. You want everything *now*!"

Then, as if my hand had become electrically charged, she pushed it away. Ruby seemed to vanish, and instead I saw the bow of a ship heading straight toward me. A towering mast leaned sharply to the side. The water around the boat was black. The vision was as vivid as though captured on film. I felt both thrilled and scared. But most of all, I was filled with anticipation of great things to come.

The boat dissolved a few seconds later when I heard Ruby's voice. She was leaning toward me, charcoal eyes intense. "I see a boat, or a yacht."

"I saw a boat too!" I cried.

Then she added, "And a big project. Something spiritual and very successful. But very difficult."

I pressed her for more details, but she dismissed me abruptly.

"Just relax," she told me. "The answers will come in time."

But I didn't relax, and day after day I wondered how and when the premonition in the shape of a vision might manifest itself. I attached an inexplicable charge to anything that had to do with boats, water, and the spiritual. I turned my camera toward all types of water-going vessels, hoping to re-create my strange vision, and in the process of taking the pictures, to uncover a clue to its origin. After I became involved with the Sword of Heaven, I still didn't feel the issue was resolved. Even though the project was clearly spiritual, there were no boats in Juan's initial story. But now, by con-necting my vision to Juan and Kazz's seagoing adventure, that all changed. The riddle had been solved.

After a moment, I managed to ask Juan if Kazz had recovered from his injuries.

"He's not well."

"So that's why he was so quick to send *me* a god," I said. "He can't place them himself."

"Perhaps," said Juan. "But why were you so quick to offer help?"

I had no simple answer and I sensed many forces at work. Clearly I was drawn to the project's vision of world peace. Very soon I would come to understand that there were other motives at work that were still unclear to me. At that moment, however, I was beginning to appreciate the full significance of the boat vision. With it, I was more prepared to act on the project. Without it, my skeptical, rational mind might have had the last word, and Juan's interesting story that first night in San Francisco would have remained just that, an interesting story followed only by dessert.

We rose to leave. Juan's final words to me were, "I've told the story of the Sword of Heaven to many people. Few responded and helped. But you…I feel as if you were waiting for it."

chapter 5

Dan on Mt. Shasta just before we
reached the summit.

There was a turtle by the name of Bert.
And Bert the Turtle was very alert.
When danger threatened him he never got hurt.
He knew just what to do.

He'd Duck and Cover. Duck and Cover.
He did what we all must learn to do.

You and you and you and you.
Duck and Cover!

—From a 1950s government "Duck and Cover" campaign

July 29, 1983. This time, I'll do it, I thought. My old childhood friend Dan Forey dozed in the car seat next to me. Right on the top. Perfect. In the distance Mount Shasta rose to 14,000 feet, its snow-tipped summit glistening in the afternoon sun.

It had been a month since I had tried to place the Shinto god at the Livermore Lab, a few weeks since my lunch with Juan Li.

Starting in my college days, I had made an annual summer pilgrimage to this majestic dormant volcano in Northern California. The first time was a late-night whim, inspired by too much beer. It ended the next morning, halfway up the mountain, when a freak lightning storm nearly killed me. Although the next five attempts to reach the summit were successful, I never again took the mountain for granted. This would be my first attempt with Dan.

"*If* I make it to the top, I'll do it," I repeated to Dan's sleeping ear, as we neared the base of the mountain. "I won't repeat what happened at the Lab."

Dan woke and whistled as the mountain filled the window. Mount Shasta seemed huge, almost ominous, and I suddenly knew that I was lying to myself. I hadn't yet figured out what had prevented me from placing the god at the Lab. Why should I be successful this time? I sensed under my resolve lurked debilitating doubts. I drove more slowly, only partially because the road had become winding and steep.

Dan and I agreed to make our ascent of Mount Shasta slowly and not macho our way up and back in one day. After hiking two-thirds of the way up, we bivouacked for the night next to Lake Helen, a grimy puddle of icy water. We placed our tent in the middle of a ring of rocks others before us built for protection from the fierce winds. We cooked a light meal, chased tiny chipmunks away from our packs, then watched the sun set. Behind us the sun turned the cliffs blood red. The valley below grew dark, and we saw the lights of the town of Mount Shasta appear below. Campfires glowed in the dark canyons. Neither Dan nor I spoke, content simply to watch the dazzling show.

Looking up at the peak from the valley below, it's easy to understand why Mount Shasta has captured the imagination of so many people through the ages. It stands snow-covered and alone, apart from the mountain ranges to the east and west, almost a perfect cone. The native peoples of California believed Mount Shasta was a holy mountain, and worshipped it in deed and lore. The early European settlers were inspired by the mountain and created stories of their own: one claims that the Lemurians, the people of the lost continent of Atlantis, dwelled within the mountain. In recent years, many New Age rites and rituals have taken place at Mount Shasta. On our ascent, Dan and I stumbled across rocks still warm from sweat lodge ceremonies and examined strange tokens of wood and feather stuck in snowbanks. At one point we even heard eerie wailing coming from the dark wooded areas below.

The sun settled below the horizon, bringing a cold darkness, and in the protection of the tent we grew chatty. I told him about Donna Rini, a woman I had just started seeing.

I met her shortly after the newspaper article appeared. We were both swimming laps at a local public pool in San Francisco. Nice suit, I told her from my lane. Yeah, right, she said sarcastically, and pushed gracefully off the wall and continued her laps. A few laps later I got her to talk. Even though I towered over her, I didn't think of her as small. She was three years older than me, quick-tongued and, true to her Italian background, expressed her emotions easily. She was an artist who worked with words and images. When she heard that I was a photographer who wrote, she told me about an art lecture on that subject by some New York artist I hadn't heard of. We made plans to attend the lecture to-gether, and things developed from there.

"Are we talking serious?" Dan asked.

"Hey, you know me!" I said. "Mr. Careful. In any case, she's thinking about moving to New York. She says all artists need to live there at least for a while. So I'm not sure where the relationship is going."

We went on to talk about childhood memories: Boy Scouts, band (he played trumpet, I played tuba), sports, and practical tricks.

"Remember the gunpowder and rockets your father

taught us to make?" he asked. "Remember the one that nearly blew up the Sellers' house?"

"And the hydrogen balloons! We're lucky we didn't kill ourselves, or someone else...." I was laughing, recalling how my father showed us how to make hydrogen by dropping bits of aluminum foil into a solution of lye and water in a soft drink bottle. The chemical reaction filled a balloon stretched over the nipple with the lighter-than-air—and extremely explosive—hydrogen.

"And the bomb shelter," Dan chimed in. "Mr. Mole!"

At the mention of the shelter I grew quiet.

While Dan reminisced about the Halloween parties we had in the bomb shelter, another memory came to me, one that I hadn't thought about in a long time: the nuclear attack drills at East Avenue Elementary School.

We'd be in the middle of something, making pumpkins for Halloween or cutting out table decorations for the Thanksgiving table. Then, suddenly, the piercing whistle! Every fire alarm at the school would ring furiously.

"The Russians have launched an attack!" we'd cry to each other. "A nuclear warhead is headed toward the Lab, toward us!"

We'd duck under desks, tables, and chairs. A thermo-nuclear holocaust could melt entire buildings down to a puddle of molten mess; still, the teacher pulled the shades over the windows to protect us from falling glass. We were too young to question the absurd logic. After a terrifying fifteen minutes, school would be declared over for the day, and we would be sent home. I would go immediately to my bedroom/bomb shelter, where my two brothers waited, big-eyed and scared. I had no idea what the other schoolchildren did. Did they go to their own shelters? What were they thinking? We never mentioned the drills to each other until we were much older; by then, the psychic wounds were so deep they were barely acknowledged.

Dan took my silence for fatigue and turned to sleep. We hadn't talked about the Shinto project but now clearly wasn't the time. I was restless. I heard huge boulders, dislodged by the quick day-to-night temperature change, tumble down the slope above us, creating huge cascades of snow and gravel. A sudden wind snapped the sides of our tent violently against the poles and rocks. I felt the intense danger of the mountain, and our smallness.

It felt as if the mountain were dying and falling on top of us. Then I remembered that Shasta is a volcano. It's not dying, I told myself. It's being born. And it may explode any minute. I started having grisly visions of what would happen if the mountain exploded. Molten rock would fry us, and nothing would be left but charred bone. Before I finally fell asleep, I reached under my head and shifted the Shinto god, which I had cushioned with a towel and my shirt. Please help me, I said silently, aware that I was communicating with the god like a child in a crib might talk to his favorite stuffed bear.

I woke suddenly to Dan lightly slapping my face. "You okay? You were yelling."

The wind had stopped, and it was calm outside. My eyes bolted open.

"Okay, okay," I gasped, struggling to pull my arms from my sleeping bag.

"You sure?" His face was alive with concern.

I shook my head. "It's okay. Sorry. Go back to sleep." As he settled back to sleep, the details of my nightmare slowly re-emerged.

I knew the dream well, but I hadn't had it for years. It had started shortly after I moved into the bomb shelter and continued on a regular basis until I left for college. Then the nightmare only occurred when I was under stress: a new relationship, a particularly hard job. Throughout the 1970s it became less and less frequent, as if it were burrowing itself deeper and deeper into my psyche. Now it was back.

It always began the same way. I am in my bedroom, the bomb shelter, alone, lying on the metal cot. There is a loud noise. It comes from the escape hatch, the one I had painted fluorescent orange.

Wham! Someone or something is knocking. I reach for the light switch, but my arm is heavy as lead. I try to move a leg but I can't. In the blackness, I sense something truly evil is outside. If I open the heavy metal door, whatever is on the other side will rush in. It will kill me, then kill my family sleeping peacefully upstairs. The pounding becomes more insistent. I want to run, but I am frozen with fear. And worse, I know the only way out is through the escape hatch—right past the evil itself. The escape hatch both protects me and prevents me from leaving. My mind and my body feel disconnected. I try to scream. Nothing.

Do something! Anything! Open the door!

No, I can't!

The nightmare always ends the same way. I awake, drenched in sweat, silently screaming.

Now, next to me, Dan was breathing easily. He was asleep. I reached behind my head, grabbed the stone god, unzipped the opening to the tent, and placed it outside on the gravel. It didn't help me after all.

I didn't sleep again that night.

When the first hint of morning light filled the tent, I shook Dan and told him to get moving. Outside, billowy clouds were already visible.

"Hurry!" I urged. I knew we would have to start now, before the day turned the snow to slush—or worse, before the clouds turned into a storm.

While Dan lashed on his crampons for footing on the icy slopes, I fumbled with the stove, boiling snow for tea.

Other climbers were already moving silently up the mountain behind our camp. We hurried through our tea and breakfast of cold milk and cereal. I packed the Shinto god along with a lunch of nuts and raisins and drinking water into my day pack. We left the tent standing, to be retrieved later in the day on our return.

In the gray dawn, we climbed for an hour until we reached a heart-shaped patch of uncovered rocks and boulders. A bank of rocks and gravel loomed ahead of us, and the peak rose beyond. Dan was breathing heavily and we rested. So far, the weather had remained unchanged. But now the clouds began to move.

"We don't have much time," I said urgently. "Let's go."

Two hours later, when we were still an hour from the summit, the storm hit. Freezing clouds filled the air with snow, and a powerful wind blew the flakes nearly horizontal to the ground. We struggled through the howling mess, determined to reach the top, but the thin mountain air forced us to take small, deliberate steps.

At the base of the summit, we smelled the sulfur springs. During a much worse storm in 1888, John Muir had immersed himself in the hot water to save his life.

"Not far now," I gasped to Dan, whose face was buried deep in his parka. I pointed into the white air. "Just over there."

We weren't a hundred yards from the summit when Dan tore back his parka and threw up, splashing tea and cereal against a frozen boulder.

He refused my offer of help, and dragged himself to the summit. In a ring of protective rocks, he lay moaning and retching, classic symptoms of altitude sickness.

Rest, I knew, wouldn't help: only a lower elevation could. I only had a few moments. I pulled the god from my pack. There has to be a crevice in the ice or a crack in the rocks, I thought. But the storm made it nearly impossible to see. The shrieking wind blew pieces of snow and ice into my face. If I ventured too far from my friend, I might never find him again.

I wanted to place the god on Mount Shasta. But how? Because of the storm, my only choice was to drop the god on the hard ice, in full view of other climbers. It would almost certainly be picked up by someone and taken back down the mountain. I was exhausted by a night without sleep, and sat down in the snow defeated.

Bad spirits!

I gripped the stone god. The storm howled around me. I could faintly hear my friend vomiting his guts out.

I tried to calm myself, to banish the thought that the storm—a common occurrence, after all—was a sign. But even as I dismissed the madness of my thoughts, I could hear a cacophony of voices—my own included—screaming:

"Turn back! Turn back from this crazy project. Turn back before it's too late."

After a few minutes, I stuffed the god into my pack and scrambled back to Dan. We quickly descended. A thousand feet lower, the clouds dissolved into blue sky and my friend revived. I looked back at the summit, now clearly visible, and wondered if I would be able to place another god again—or if I even dared to try.

After I returned home to San Francisco, despite my failures to place the second god, I clung to my initial belief that the Sword of Heaven was a meaningful peace project. I took Juan Li's advice and sent three gods with sympathetic friends to distant places—and one with a man who responded to the newspaper article. For the next few months the placing of the gods went smoothly.

Nadav Elder, an Israeli who studied architecture in San Francisco, took one to the Sea of Galilee. He brought home color pictures of himself in a tiny boat in the middle of the sea, with the god's cloth wrapping around his head.

Julie Christensen, the friend who was having lunch with me when the package of gods appeared on my porch in San Francisco, took one to the mouth of the Mississippi River. In a letter she wrote to Kazz, she explained that Atchafalaya swamp near Baton Rouge, Louisiana, is one of the last great swamps of the Mississippi river basin. "While everyone else went fishing, my brother and I took a small boat into the swamp. The canals are winding and intersecting, sometimes only eight or ten feet wide. Finally the trees parted and we entered Lake Bigeux, a relatively deep body of water where several canals and bays converge. We selected a spot in the center of the lake and left our package there. It was a hot, humid day, and my brother decided to swim a bit before we headed home. He dove from the boat and surfaced with a strange expression—the water was cold! Fifteen feet from the boat in any direction the water was very warm, as it usually is, but right around us it was very cold. I suppose there was a spring below us, but I have never heard of springs in the swamp. It is here we placed the god. The story of your efforts has touched the hearts of a great variety of people. I am pleased and honored to have participated in my small way. Good luck to you."

Lynn Ferrin, a magazine editor in San Francisco, placed a god in Canada. After a two-day dog sled ride, she placed it in the Athabasca River in western Canada, within Jasper National Park in the province of Alberta. The river runs almost 800 miles from the mountains across the plains to Lake Athabasca. In the lake, the waters mingle with the waters of the Peace River system and ultimately reach the Arctic Ocean through the Mackenzie River system. Lynn threw the god in at a spot with a beautiful view of the snowcapped mountain range to the west. "It was wonderful to take part in this project," she wrote, "and I hope that the spirit of the god travels a long way in the far north."

Hugh Leddy, a broadcast engineer from Chugiak, Alaska, envisioned placing a god while Zen monks, Buddhist priests, and a TV crew participated in a sort of media event. I sent him a god, but his ambitious plans fell through; he finally ended up placing the god quietly in a bay near Homer with his wife and children and some kayakers who happened by.

"The first impression I got, even as I stood in front of the little country post office in Chugiak was that what I was holding, even before I opened the paper-wrapped, brown cardboard box that held it, was emanating a gentle and benign but quite awesome impression of *strength*... I felt I had just been handed a trust—a mantle of responsibility had in some way come to me...it was up to me to ensure the *kami* arrived at whatever place turned out to be its intended destination.

"Originally, I had planned to take the *kami* to Little Diomede, an island in the Bering Sea that is only three miles away from another island called Big Diomede which is part of Russia. Nothing happened as planned.

"Once we got to Land's End on the Homer Spit, the wind was biting cold—and, apart from ourselves, the beach was deserted. It was the end of the season and the charter and tour boat businesses had folded in their shutters, locked up, and gone home. There was no means available to take the *kami* any farther. Two kayakers, Willy Stark and Meg Kurtagh of Homer, Alaska, were about to take off to paddle across the deep water. There was no room for me either in his kayak or hers. Reluctantly, realizing I was but one link along a chain, I agreed to let them paddle out and place the *kami* where it had to go. I took pictures from the beach. Thanks for trusting me with one Shinto god."

Like me, Hugh learned the project wasn't as simple as it seemed. It had a mind of its own.

PART TWO

Conflict within
weakens the power
to conquer danger
without.

chapter 6

Kazz praying at the shrine.

On August 31, 1983, the Soviets shot down Korean flight 007, killing all 269 people onboard. President Reagan responded by calling the USSR an "evil empire," even though the flight had strayed into Soviet airspace. In the early fall, NATO launched a major exercise called "Able Archer 83." The Soviets thought this was a precursor to a major attack and prepared a major offensive of their own. Were these the sparks that would set off the next world war?

November 19, 1983: In my dream that first night in Tokyo, Kazz was behind me, and I could sense him smiling with pride. In a misty, featureless foreground I perceived four or five ghostly figures dressed in white robes. They were hurling

long, vicious daggers at me. But ten feet before me, the daggers turned into dinner knives, the kind with dull, rounded
tips. I easily deflected them from my body with my hands,
and they fell harmlessly to the ground. I didn't feel fear or
concern. Rather, I felt awkward, as if something were happening that I didn't understand—as though I were part of a
game for which I didn't know the rules.

I awoke from my puzzling dream in the tiny hotel room.
I didn't know what time it was. My internal body clock said
midmorning, California time, but the darkness outside reminded me I was at the Asia Center Hotel in Tokyo, in the
middle of the night—only a few days away from finally
meeting the mysterious Kazz and his venerable teacher.

I heard Donna stir and then roll over on her side. Our
relationship had evolved a lot since I had told my friend Dan
about her on Mount Shasta four months earlier. Not only
did we share the swimming pool, art, and bed, but when I
told her about the Shinto project she was intrigued. She saw
it as a wonderful performance piece, and the Shinto priest
who had started it as an artist in his own right. All it needed,
she said, was a Philip Glass score. In November, when I asked
if she'd join me on a trip to Japan, she didn't hesitate. She had
been fascinated with Japan for a long time, and was curious
to meet the man behind the Sword of Heaven project.

It was raining lightly, typical autumn weather in central
Japan. Restless, I clicked on my reading light and quietly
opened my briefcase to reread the letter I had received from

Kazz a few weeks earlier. His back was better, and he was once again placing gods.

"I just came back to Japan after I have placed the gods in three places, Madras, Colombo, and Mauritius Island. We have 40 Gods left. My teacher is concerned. Time is short. If it is possible for you to come to Japan before the 23rd of November, please write. We have a special ceremony then."

I shook my head, placing the letter on the table. "He's right about time being short," I thought. "The world is more dangerous than ever."

I had rationalized our trip to this expensive Asian archipelago in a number of ways: a photo project, a travel story, a book promotion. But in all honesty, Kazz's invitation was all I needed. I owed it to myself and the others who had placed gods through me to meet the people behind this ambitious project, even if the trip were a financial bust.

I heard Donna call out, "I'm wide awake! What time is it?"

"Four," I said, gently stroking her cheek. "Eleven in the morning California time. We've got hours until sunrise."

I hugged her and held her for a long time.

"Careful. My stomach. I knew I shouldn't have eaten the duck they served on the plane."

And then she stretched, her arms nearly touching the two walls of our tiny room.

"I can't go back to sleep," she said. "What shall we do?"

I knew from my last trip to Japan, eight years earlier, that the only place open at this hour was the Tsuki fish market. I suggested that we go there.

The streets were empty, and there was little sign of the massive human energy that transformed Tokyo from the rubble and ruin at the end of World War II into a gleaming, modern city, one of the most populous in the world. At the fish market we joined a few other blurry-eyed foreigners among the throng of Japanese fishmongers strolling around the vast indoor 50-acre marketplace. There was every type of fish imaginable for sale, in every form: frozen, dried, or freshly cleaned. The waters surrounding the four main islands that make up Japan are fertile, but the huge tuna and whales obviously came from the far corners of the world. We passed a stand oozing the smell of fish broth.

"I'm not sure this was a good idea," Donna said, still nauseated from our in-flight meal.

By then it was 7 a.m. and the sun was rising, brightening the gray Tokyo sky. We went out into the now-crowded streets to find a bus back to our hotel.

There, Donna went for tea, while I went up to our room to call Kazz. A woman answered the phone. In seconds Kazz was on the phone welcoming Donna and me to Japan. His voice was cheerful, but his English slow and careful.

"The ceremony is on Wednesday. I'll meet you at the station in a couple days, on Tuesday," he said. Then he gave me directions. We were to meet him south of Tokyo, three hours by the Shinkansen, or bullet train. Just hearing Kazz's voice on the phone thrilled me. There is a real person behind the letters, I thought. And I'm going to finally meet him!

It was twilight when we arrived at Kashiharajingumae, a small train station between Nara and Osaka. We were met by neon advertisements blasting messages about donuts and burgers. Into this chaotic scene walked a man wearing a jogging suit, his long black hair wild as if he had just finished a long run. He called out my name, mispronouncing it. It was Kazz.

I don't remember if we bowed. Our meeting seemed so Western, with him in a jogging suit surrounded by fast-food joints. I just grabbed his hand and shook it. After I introduced Donna, Kazz grew silent, donning an impassive Asian public countenance. He gripped our baggage and led us to his car.

"It's old," he apologized.

"What? The car?" I joked. At most it was three years old.

"The Japanese don't like used things. We were given it as a gift."

The silence returned. Donna climbed in back, and I sat on the left, where in America the driver's seat would be. In

Japan the driver sits on the right, British-style. In the awk-
wardness of our continued silence, I wanted to grab the nonexistent wheel.

Finally Kazz broke the silence as we drove away from the
station. "There is much to tell."

I was relieved. I hadn't known how to handle his silence,
and I was dying to talk. "Where are we going?" I asked.

"Tonight the teacher is preparing for tomorrow's ceremony. The mountain is only an hour's drive."

What mountain? Juan never mentioned a mountain. I
sensed a widening gap between Kazz and me, and I wanted
to fill it with answers as fast as possible. At that moment,
however, I knew intuitively that I needed to restrain myself.

"Was that your wife who answered the phone?" I asked
instead.

"Yes."

"What does she think of all your travel?" Donna asked
from the backseat.

"She understands." Kazz managed a smile, as he half
turned to her. "Most of the time."

The small town and its neon melted into darkness behind
us. We followed narrow cobblestone roads past smaller towns
and villages divided by dark patches of what I assumed were
rice fields. Even though we were far from the intense urban
density of Tokyo, the countryside felt carefully shaped and
planned out. Nothing seemed out of place, not a single

cobblestone. An hour later we began climbing a steep mountain road.

"This is Mount Katsuragi. Soon we arrive at Tenkenjinja, the shrine of the Sword of Heaven," Kazz said, as he twisted the steering wheel to follow the sharp curves in the road. "The teacher is waiting."

At the mention of the teacher, I felt a childlike eagerness and impatience. My vision of him was pure fantasy, a high lama of Shangri-la, old, frail, and wrinkled. I've always loved James Hilton's *Lost Horizon*, the book that introduced Shangri-la to the world. Perhaps I'd be like Conway, the book's main character, and the teacher would reveal some marvelous secret that would change my life.

"How did you meet him?" I asked.

Maybe Kazz was deliberately trying to sustain the drama to make our meeting more mysterious, because he didn't answer. Instead, he said simply, "Please wait."

We were silent a long time. Then Donna, bless her heart, said, "At least tell us his name." Her vision of the teacher clearly was more objective than mine. She saw him as a talented artist creating a masterpiece and therefore very human. She had her feet planted firmly on the ground while I floated in a cloud of fantasy.

Kazz gripped the steering wheel tightly. "Hakuryu Takizawa."

"Hakuryu Takizawa?" she repeated.

"Hakuryu means White Dragon. Takizawa is his family name," Kazz said. Before she could say anything more he pulled the car to the side of the road. "Here we are."

It was dark, but we could faintly see a valley far below. I saw the black outline of a crow sitting on a bare late-autumn branch. The new moon was just emerging over the hillside terraces. The darkness began to glow with a dull silver sheen.

"It's late," I said.

"No problem," replied Kazz as he opened the car door and led us down a steep path to a dimly lit house.

The man who watched us walk through the door was no frail lama. He leapt from the floor, moving quickly across the tatami mats, and put out his hand in a hearty Western-style greeting.

"*Yokuirashaimashita!*" he said in a deep voice, welcoming us in Japanese. He was slender and tall, approaching my own height of six feet. He was wearing a white, two-piece garment: a long skirt under a robe-length coat. His eyes were piercing. They darted between me and Donna with the happiness of a grandfather seeing his grandchildren for the first time, without the sagelike reserve that I had expected, especially after Kazz's reticence.

He greeted Donna by clasping her small hand carefully between both of his and smiling deeply at the same time.

He turned to his student and spoke rapidly in Japanese. Kazz motioned us toward the center of the room, where a kerosene heater glowed warmly. There was also a cooking pit with coals that filled the room with steam and the smell of food.

The room was large and open, and in the back, in the shadow of the kerosene heater, two figures came towards us. One was an older woman, her head bowed as she walked forward; the other was a tall young man. The teacher's wife and son offered polite greetings, and then returned to the back of the room where they had been sleeping.

"Do they live here?" I asked Kazz.

"Nobody lives here. They just stay here before ceremonies. The teacher lives nearby, in Osaka."

I was anxious to ask the teacher questions about the Sword of Heaven, but to do so at this point seemed hasty. Instead, we spent the next fifteen minutes in casual conversation, with Kazz translating.

"Do you want some broth?" the teacher asked, pointing to a black pot full of boiling liquid, unrecognizable vegetables, and glutinous rice.

I accepted and it tasted wonderful. Donna, however, declined. The teacher looked concerned, but Donna reassured him that it had nothing to do with the broth, that her stomach was upset from something she ate and she was sure it would be fine soon.

The teacher asked if I had been to Japan before, and I told him only once, when I was researching a book on bathing customs. Pleased that I had taken such an interest in one of the great passions of the Japanese people, he told us that we mustn't miss the southern island, Kyushu, where people lie on the beach and have themselves covered with sand heated by volcanic water.

When the teacher asked me how old I was, I learned that Kazz and I were the same age, 31. The teacher told us that according to the Chinese calendar, we were both dragons.

"What does being a dragon mean?" I asked.

"Both of you are very stubborn," he replied with a knowing smile.

Then the teacher asked if Donna and I were married.

I told him no, we weren't married. We'd only been together for five months. I briefly wondered if our unwed intimacy would offend him, but it didn't seem to. He replied that we looked like brother and sister, which surprised me when I considered Donna's Italian background in contrast to my Nordic one. It also struck me as an odd comment, especially since I was sleeping with her. I felt a little defensive until he explained, "Your souls. You both have *yasai*, gentle souls."

Although the teacher exchanged glances with both Donna and me, his questions, including the one about us being married or not, were focused mostly toward me. Donna was content to sit back and just listen. I was confident that later, when we were alone, I could count on her as a reality-check. She'd be able to temper my judgment with more detached reasoning.

When Kazz suggested that now would be a good time to ask the teacher about the project, I sat up straight.

"First, tell the teacher that I am honored to help with his peace project, even in such a small way," I said to Kazz.

The teacher smiled and nodded when Kazz translated my English into Japanese. "But it's not my project. It is the project of God. We may think differently, but it is God who put us in contact with one another."

Kazz leaned toward the teacher and asked him to repeat something, then he turned back to me. "Are you a Christian?"

I'd never been asked that question so directly before. "I'm not involved with any organized religion," I replied.

As a child I had attended Livermore's Unitarian Church. Sunday services often meant a field trip to the Rosicrucian Museum in nearby San Jose, or to the planetarium in San Francisco's Golden Gate Park rather than a stuffy church sermon. I had always held Christianity at arm's length, but a Unitarian, I suspected, wouldn't have had any trouble with me sitting in that room, discussing and sharing religious ideas with a Shinto priest. They might even have invited the priest to come talk in their own church.

"At least I'm not involved now," I, added since I hadn't

been to a Unitarian service since I was eleven or twelve years old.

"I've never had much interest in Christianity," the teacher said bluntly.

He looked carefully for my reaction. I didn't say anything, nervously scratching behind my ear.

The teacher smiled.

"Many Christian missionaries come to Japan. They talk from their head. They feel empty inside. They don't have any personal power."

Again, he looked at me carefully before continuing.

"They call themselves Christians, but they confuse me. Jesus Christ is another one of God's projects, a gift to the human world from God. *He* has much power."

He spoke in the present tense, and I mentioned that to Kazz.

"He met Jesus during one of our ceremonies," Kazz said casually.

I shifted my legs uncomfortably under me. "He met Jesus Christ?"

"Yes. He left his body and his spirit traveled to Tibet. That's where all the great teachers live—Buddha, Mohammed, Confucius…Christ."

I looked over at Donna, who I knew had been raised Catholic but didn't formally practice it anymore. She looked as puzzled as I felt. The teacher caught my glance, nodded and said: "Yes, I was very impressed with Jesus. He taught me about the Great Love, how God protects not only some of the people or some of the world, but gives love to all humankind."

I didn't know how to respond. I was thrown off by how casually the teacher had brought up out-of-body travel, as if it were a completely natural thing for him to do. I was also surprised that the simplest of all of Christ's messages—to love unconditionally—was a radically new concept for him. Yet I was deeply impressed that he had cut right to what I considered the essence of Christ's teachings.

"Yes," I said slowly, "There's a big difference between Christ's teachings and a lot of organized Christianity. But please don't judge all Christians by the acts of a few."

"The same with Shinto!" the teacher exclaimed. "Many people think of World War II when they think of Shinto."

The teacher settled back, putting his bowl away.

"That is such a small part of our long history, the War. Bad spirits were in control." Now he spoke softly, with heaviness in his voice. "Long ago, in the beginning, Shinto didn't even have a name. But then Buddhism, Confucianism, and Christianity came to us from the outside world. These religions had books and dogma. In response, our leaders commissioned a written chronicle of the ancient legends, which became known as the *Kojiki*. They also commanded a name be given to it: Shinto, or the way of the gods."

The teacher sat up. "But I am afraid that by giving it a name, we lost the original spirit of Shinto. We caged a powerful bird. During World War II, the bird became sick. Did you know what MacArthur did after he stripped the emperor of his divinity?" the teacher asked. "He outlawed the possession of swords!"

I had forgotten that detail. At that moment the thought struck me as comical.

My country had just blasted two of Japan's major cities to radioactive dust, and we were scared of swords?

"But the sword represented militarism, like the swastika in Nazi Germany," I offered, perhaps a little apologetically.

"Then, yes," said the teacher. "But the sword also represents positive action. In any case, the sword is only one symbol of Shinto. The jewel, which represents the heart, and the mirror, which represents knowledge, are others. When all three of these divine treasures—the sword, the jewel, and the mirror—are worshipped and understood, man is complete."

I asked the teacher what he did during the war. I carefully phrased the question so that he could, if he wanted, gracefully decline.

"I was in Manchuria," he replied easily. "I was a commissary clerk." I assumed that this meant he didn't see any action, or more bluntly, that he didn't kill anyone.

Then the teacher asked me, just as carefully, if I had relatives who fought in the war with Japan.

"A family friend. On my mother's side," I replied. "He was killed at Pearl Harbor."

There was an awkward silence. In all honesty, I didn't

know much about the guy. I remembered only that my American grandmother once told me about visiting Hawaii and placing flowers on his grave.

After a long pause, he said, "Before, I prayed to the God of Japan. Now I never pray to the God of Japan. I pray to the God of the Universe, *Ameno-Minakanushi-no-kami*, or to the Sun Goddess, *Amaterasu-Omikami*."

At this statement, Kazz stopped translating and looked at the teacher intently.

"What?" I asked, noting his concern.

"This is a very radical idea," Kazz said finally.

"Including the rest of the world in his prayers?"

Kazz glanced at the teacher but didn't translate. He turned back to me. "The idea of placing Shinto gods beyond Japanese soil is hard for many people to understand or accept. Even within our group, only a few people know."

I pulled back, once again totally confused.

"What about the project?" I asked. "It isn't just about saving Japan, is it? It's about saving the entire world, right?"

"Of course."

At this point the teacher yawned. His wife was already asleep on a tatami mat. Donna's eyes were closing. "Soon it will be dawn," said Kazz, impassively, ignoring my troubled look. "Translating is very tiring. You can ask the teacher more questions later."

Donna and I were given separate futons and bedding, which we placed next to each other in a corner of the room.

I wanted to ask Donna what she thought but she was already asleep. I lay on the cushioned floor, staring at the wooden rafters. For the moment I felt satisfied. So what if the teacher hadn't fulfilled my fantasies—at least he wasn't a religious extremist. In fact, both Kazz and the teacher seemed like sincere and reasonable people. Hey, he was open-minded enough to evoke Jesus Christ! Then I remembered the out-of body travel and the fact that the project was secret from most of the teacher's followers. Before I fell asleep, I had a strong sense that the deeper I delved into the project the less I would understand.

chapter 7

The teacher welcoming a follower
to the Mount Katsuragi shrine.

*"Immediately upon hearing the news of Hiroshima, sensitive
thinkers had realized that doomsday—an idea that until then had
seemed like a religious or science-fiction myth, something outside
worldly time—would become as real a part of the possible future as
tomorrow's breakfast."*

—*Nuclear Fear: A History of Images*, by Spencer R. Weart

We woke to a brilliant fall day. The dark night shadows behind the shrine disappeared, becoming yellow and red leaves,
and the cold morning air suddenly turned warm as the sun
reached past the rice terraces to strike the freshly plowed
field below.

I peered out the doorway and saw the teacher. He had changed into an ornate kimono, a plumed headdress, and a pair of black wooden shoes that added at least eight inches to his height. He was standing near a red wooden gate or torii, which looked somewhat like a football goal post with an extra beam on the top. A huge twisted rope, or *shime-nawa*, dangled from the two vertical beams.

The teacher was now transformed into the exotic figure I had imagined back in San Francisco. Here now was Gandalf or Merlin, a true wizard. However, my fantasy was dashed when I looked beyond the teacher and saw his congregation of about a hundred people coming down the narrow path. They were dressed in Western suits and Sunday dresses. They looked so normal. The teacher greeted everyone cheerfully, not unlike a midwestern Presbyterian minister greeting his parish.

Past the torii, in front of a rectangular lawn, was the shrine itself. Fifteen rows of folding chairs faced the outdoor shrine. There were five steps that led to the top of the base of the shrine, all made of stone. The base was about the size of a small room and about four feet high. In the middle of it was another, narrower, chimneylike stone pedestal, also about four feet high. On top of this was an elaborate miniature wood building with a slanted roof and protruding beams that crossed each other to form a V at the top. Inside this building, out of sight, was a *kami*, according to Kazz. In front of the building, set on wooden tables at the top of the steps, were offerings to the *kami* of salt, sake, and fruit. Today's ceremony was to celebrate the ninth anniversary of the shrine.

After they greeted the teacher, the people in the procession rinsed their mouths and poured water over their fingertips at a stone basin set up outside the wooden torii in ritualistic purification.

Kazz had changed into a suit and tie and was sipping a cup of tea.

"What will the teacher tell the people about me and Donna?" I asked, dressing quickly because I could see that the ceremony would start soon. I was very glad that I had learned on my previous visit to Japan to bring formal clothes, so I had a jacket and tie ready. Donna always wore urban black, and this occasion was no exception. "Won't they be curious what brought us here?"

"Not everyone needs things answered as quickly as you."

An attractive woman and three little girls broke away from the group gathered in front of the teacher and waved to us.

"My wife Tazuko and my children," Kazz explained.

The young girls clung tenaciously to Tazuko's leg, hiding their heads in her skirt.

"They've never seen foreigners before," Kazz's wife said apologetically after we were introduced. "Except on television."

While they walked back toward the teacher and the

shrine, I hastily wrapped a tie around my neck and joined
Donna, who was waiting for me just outside the torii.

The ceremony started and like in my dream that first
night in Tokyo, I had no idea what was going on. Every
movement of the teacher and his assistants became deliberate
and slow. There was chanting and praying, and during the
prayers, Kazz told me, the teacher made many references to
world peace. During much of the ceremony, we sat on the
chairs along with everyone else. I sat toward the front with
Kazz, and Donna sat in the back with Tazuko. Toward the
end of the ceremony, each member of the congregation—in
pairs—took leafy branches with strips of white linen tied to
them and laid them as offerings at the base of the shrine.

I walked forward with Kazz and placed a branch on the
altar as well. One of the teacher's assistants waved a wand of
white paper, called *haraigushi*, over each of us, purifying us.
First he flicked the *haraigushi* over the left shoulder of the
kneeled person, then the right shoulder, and then he repeated the motion with a strong flourish. Donna and Kazz's
wife followed behind us. When it was Donna's turn, she knelt
and then turned and gave me a wink.

Finally, after everyone had made an offering to the *kami*,
the entire group turned toward the north, toward the imper-

ial palace in Tokyo, and shouted out a hearty banzai, the traditional greeting of health and long life to the emperor. Donna and I stood looking quizzically at each other. We knew that Shinto was no longer the state religion, and that the emperor had been stripped of his divinity after World War II. Kazz told me later that they were just showing respect to the emperor who remains their spiritual leader.

Afterward we all threw rice in the direction of the shrine, as if the ceremony were a Western wedding and the shrine was both the bride and groom. Then box lunches were distributed that contained sticky balls of rice filled with vegetables, tiny portions of fish and a round, succulent fruit that tasted like a cross between a pear and an apple. We ate the delicious food on the grass in front of the shrine in the ceremonial area.

To a shopkeeper, an import/export man, a craftsman, and a gardener who walked up to us as we ate, I was introduced by Kazz as a visiting American journalist, Donna as my wife. They said a few words and strolled away.

"No one really cares if you are actually married or not," whispered Kazz, "but in Japan appearance is very important."

Now the teacher walked up, looking completely at ease in his long robe and large hat.

"You are both invited to his home in Osaka the day after tomorrow," Kazz translated. "I told him you would come."

I looked worried, wondering how we were going to get there.

"I'll take you. In the meantime, please stay at my house."

Kazz drove back from the mountain, but this time three little girls and Tazuko were crammed in the car as well. Even though the overloaded car listed dangerously around each curve, neither Kazz nor his wife nor the children seemed to notice. Donna and I, however, glanced at each other nervously.

"We live not far, in Gose," said Kazz. "We wanted to live near the shrine."

It was a four-room house with a kitchen, a living room, and two bedrooms upstairs. One bedroom was full of books and antiques, which meant that the entire family lived in the other three rooms. Donna and I found a corner near a bookcase and dropped our luggage.

In the tiny kitchen, Tazuko prepared fresh noodles sent by her parents, who owned a noodle factory. The living room was cold, but we sat and ate around a low table with a built-in infrared heater. The noodles were perfectly cooked and tasted wonderful. Tazuko explained that her parents only used organic flour so they were safe from all pesticides and other contaminants. At first our conversation with Kazz and Tazuko was awkward; we struggled to find common subjects of interest. The girls were quiet and just stared at us, barely touching their noodles. Then Kazz told us about his interest in jazz—when he was younger he played the bass—and we were all on familiar ground.

After the meal, Tazuko cleaned up and Kazz went upstairs. "To pray," his wife explained.

Before we fell asleep, the children came into our room, rosy red from a hot bath, and giggled "Good night" to us in English. We slept in the "library"; the rest of the family slept in one bed.

We couldn't sleep. A bright light from outside filled the tiny room, and we could hear the children tossing and turning, and outside an occasional car driving noisily along the cobblestone road.

Noise and light have always been especially irritating to me: After moving out of the bomb shelter, I have always sought basement bedrooms that duplicated its tomblike serenity. Sleeping anywhere else has always been difficult.

Donna reached for the earplugs she always carried.

"You want a pair?" she whispered, knowing all about my sleep problems.

When she first had heard that I was raised in a bomb shelter she had howled in laughter. It was funny. Her boyfriend was a troglodyte! But then I reminded her of the circumstances—the Cuban missile crisis, the duck and cover drills, the fear of instant death—and she understood. Her father was a captain in the Air Force, and she was an Air Force brat, moving from base to base. She always called him "Sir." In 1962, when she was thirteen years old, her father was stationed in Salina, Kansas, as part of the Strategic Air Command (SAC). He was a navigator aboard a B-52 bomber loaded with nuclear bombs. In October, a red alert was called, and suddenly all the fathers disappeared from the base. The moms were tense, and Donna and the other children felt surrounded by suppressed hysteria. She said she held the memory in her gut.

"I don't need the plugs right now," I whispered back. "I need to talk."

"About what?"

"The ceremony, the teacher, Kazz, everything. What did you think?"

"Well, Kazz reminds me of my ex-husband. He seems really difficult."

"Difficult?"

"Yeah. He has his hands tightly on the wheel. He's very careful."

"And the teacher?" I asked.

"He's wonderful," she answered. "I really like him."

"I don't know…" I said.

"What?" she asked, turning to look at me in the glow of the streetlight. "You don't know what?"

"Why is the project secret? Why doesn't Kazz and his teacher tell the others in the group? You know I don't like secrets."

Donna knew that my father's work at the Lab was highly classified, and that I always resented the fact that he couldn't tell us what he did.

After a moment Donna said carefully, "There's probably a good explanation. But in the meantime, why don't you relax? This is really special. We're in Japan! We're lucky to be here."

"Yeah, I guess you're right," I answered.

I knew one thing. I was honestly happy to be with Donna in Japan. I had some doubts when I first asked her to go. Six weeks traveling together seemed like a long time. It was early in the trip but so far so good. We traveled well together. Then I remembered the teacher's comment about us being brother and sister. Even though he had qualified it, saying it was our souls that were related, it still bothered me. Did he doubt the passion of our relationship? Did he see something I didn't? Okay, so I did have a few reservations about the relationship. For one thing, she kept talking about moving to New York. And when it came to the ins and outs of relationships, she was so self-assured. No doubt about it, she was more experienced than I. She'd been married, divorced, had done the therapy thing. When we talked about ways to make things work, I was always feeling a bit left behind, a bit inadequate. But it would work out. It always did, didn't it? Suddenly I felt claustrophobic and my heart tightened.

"Were you offended when the teacher called us brother and sister?" I asked her.

"No, were you?"

"I thought it was rather strange, that's all."

"Well then, as your older sister," she said, handing me the earplugs, "I say 'go to sleep.'"

We spent the next day in Gose. On a stroll around town, while Donna remained at home with Tazuko and the kids, I learned how Kazz had become involved with the Sword of Heaven. He told me that it was indeed Juan Li who made him curious about Shinto. After he returned from Kashmir, at a used bookstore in Tokyo, Kazz chanced upon a rare book about Shinto by a man named Tomokiyo. The author described Iwakiyama, a sacred mountain located in southern Japan where he had founded a monastery. Kazz was so intrigued by the book that he made a special pilgrimage to the mountain monastery. There, Kazz learned that Tomokiyo had died in 1952, but had passed on his knowledge to a group of disciples. One of the disciples was Hakuryu Takizawa, the White Dragon, whom Kazz quickly befriended. Soon he became his disciple.

During our time together, I also got a sense of Kazz's ambivalence toward modern Japan. We stopped at a grocery store in the center of the small town. At the cash register in front of us was a small boy buying a candy bar, dressed in a cute school uniform with matching shorts, jacket, and cap.

Kazz caught my inquisitive look. "*We* never wore fancy uniforms. We couldn't afford them."

We walked past an electronics store, well-stocked for such a small town.

Kazz sighed. "I met a Japanese girl on a plane headed to Los Angeles. Do you know why she was going to L.A.? To shop! I tried to tell her about Shinto, about the spirit world. She wasn't interested."

After a moment he said, "A lot of things are different now. And not all of them are good."

On that same walk, I asked Kazz more about the monastery in southern Japan. I was unclear exactly what the relationship was between Kazz's teacher Takizawa and the other disciples. If they were all disciples of Tomokiyo, the founder of the monastery, why then was Takizawa teaching here, in the north, so far away?

"To be frank," Kazz answered, "the other teachers see him as a bit of a renegade."

"What? They don't like him sending Shinto gods outside of Japan?" I asked.

"They don't know about the project," he said.

"It's a secret from them too?"

Kazz was silent, and instead of giving me an answer, he just turned and looked at me impassively. It was becoming a familiar look. As I shrugged my shoulders, I wondered if he was purposefully playing with my head. Did he enjoy frustrating me with his vague and incomplete answers? I was getting tired of this game, and if Kazz wanted me to keep playing, he better tell me all the rules, quick.

The next day it was time to visit the teacher in Osaka. Kazz drove us to his home, a modest suburban house with a simple Japanese garden. The teacher greeted us at the door and first invited us into a Western-style living room complete with a couch, a coffee table, and a TV. After a few minutes of casual conversation, we stepped behind a set of shoji screens and sat in a room filled with traditional tatami mats and incongruously lit by fluorescent lights.

I had brought several bottles of Jack Daniel's whiskey from the States, a gift I knew was much appreciated in Japan. I handed one of the bottles to the teacher. He graciously accepted it and passed it on to his wife, who took it and our coats to another room. Later I saw a cupboard full of various whiskies, gifts appreciated but untouched.

As in our first meeting several days earlier, our conversation followed a circuitous route before arriving at the topic of the Sword of Heaven. We discussed Donna's and my itinerary. We talked about Japanese bathing customs, and we talked about the teacher's son. We even talked about the weather.

The moment the project came up, Kazz shifted his legs underneath him. He pulled his back up straight. The teacher's voice changed, becoming deeper and more deliberate. Occasionally he looked thoughtfully into space.

The teacher reached for a globe sitting nearby, covered with red-topped pins. He proudly showed us where the gods had been placed. I could see a pin in the spot where I placed a god in Norway and one in Taiwan where Juan Li had been. Europe was well covered, including London, Paris, Helsinki, and Athens. So was China and Southeast Asia. Kazz had placed a god in Antarctica, but there were none in southern Africa. Gods had been placed in the Panama Canal; as well as Peru and Chile but none elsewhere in South America.

I stared at the globe and for the first time really appreciated the magnitude of the project. The teacher had already accomplished so much, and yet there was so much left to be done. I asked the teacher where he got the idea for the project in the first place.

"It was the 11th of May, 1954," he remembered, "when I was instructed by God to go to the top of Takachiho mountain in southern Japan, on the island of Kyushu."

On the mountain, the teacher said he made spiritual contact with Tomokiyo, the man whose book had led Kazz to the mountain monastery. Tomokiyo had died two years before, but his spirit gave Takizawa instructions to go into solitary prayer and meditation for 1,000 days.

"Over three years. What patience!" I whistled.

"The teacher's wife brought him food once a week, but he didn't talk to her or anyone else the whole time," Kazz added. "That's when he had the vision to move to Osaka and build a shrine here on Mount Katsuragi and to both teach and begin the project."

"And how do you know where to place the gods?" I asked. "Do you have a plan?"

"God always gives one a sense of control," the teacher said. "So if one day you say to yourself: I want this or I want that, this is a message from God. God has made contact, and you know."

I recalled my attempts to place a god at the Lab and my adventures on Mount Shasta with my terrible dream. Perhaps the teacher could explain why it was so difficult. Had I picked bad spots?

"The place wasn't the problem," he answered. "Bad spirits always make the problem. If you had been successful, these places would have become very important places for peace.

"Bad spirits had to do something," he continued, "like make a storm or give you bad dreams. There are always bad spirits who want to interfere with our work for peace. Our actions and prayers weaken the power of these bad spirits."

Donna, who had been listening quietly, now leaned

toward me. "Are you sure you really wanted to place them?" she asked.

I looked at her intently. "I'm not sure of anything."

I had been wondering since I first heard about the project how the teacher broke the sword into so many pieces and how he embedded them in stone. I didn't dare look inside. First, it seemed wrong. And, besides, they were tightly sealed, and it would have taken a chisel to break them open. I received an enigmatic answer when I asked.

"It's very difficult to say what is inside the stone," he answered and then paused for a long time.

"But is it metal, from a blade?"

"The stone is the mental body of the sword. For 3,000 years we have had a method, called *chinkon*, of making the body of God."

"So it's not really an actual piece of sword inside the stone?" I asked, directing my question to Kazz.

"Yes, it is," replied Kazz. "And at the same time, no it isn't."

"But there are really only 108 pieces?"

Kazz shot me a funny look. "Where did you get that number?" he asked, not bothering to translate my question for the teacher.

"From Juan."

"This 108 is not a Shinto number. It's a Buddhist number."

"Well, how many gods are there then?"

"Something like 108."

Okay, I thought, one more contradiction to consider. Would I ever get the details right? It didn't look like I could. Maybe I should take Donna's advice and relax and not let the details mess up a good story.

We talked for about an hour. The teacher complained that countries were obsessed with themselves: they had forgotten the needs and concerns of other countries. Humankind had forgotten to pray and there was a price to pay. He called the earth one big home, a "small shrine of the highest God of the universe." He said we really didn't need individual countries but "small groups, like states."

Then like a father giving friendly paternal advice, the teacher told me that I should live abroad. It would be good for me to get away from the United States for a while. I appreciated his advice and found myself craving more, wanting to be told what to do by someone older and wiser.

Near the end, I apologized for asking too many questions, although in fact I had many more.

"It's okay," said the teacher. "When man has questions he has power."

At the end, the teacher stood. Donna and I stiffly followed suit.

"Each land has its own gods," he said looking at both Donna and me, "but because of bad spirits, it is difficult for them to connect. When we put the body of God—the Sword of Heaven—around the world, the vibration of this body of God makes a loop around the earth. This network makes the God work easier in the human world.

"This meeting has been very important," the teacher said as he motioned us to the door. "Each of us gets a vibration from the God world. As we understand each other, our minds become one. Remember, when you meet anyone, you are meeting the body of God. Man is God's embodiment. Every evil arises when he forgets this."

On the way out we stopped for a moment in the living room where I asked the teacher one final question. "Should I try placing a god on Shasta or at the Livermore Lab again?"

"First you have to get more power," the teacher replied. "Then you can put the gods in the same place."

"And how do I get this power?" I asked.

"Some day you must visit Iwakiyama," he said. "At the mountain monastery many interesting things are taught. There you may get the power you need. I will see that you are welcome."

Finally we left, and Kazz drove us to the train station. Donna and I carried two-week train passes for unlimited travel in Japan.

We followed a suggestion from the teacher's wife and traveled to the southern island of Kyushu. There we spent two weeks exploring the rugged coast and the sharp, craggy inland mountains. We quickly noticed that the area was much less populated than the rest of Japan. The hotels and food were cheaper, and the people were more relaxed and friendly. At the southernmost part of the island, in Ibusuki, we found the *tsunaburo*, or sand baths that teacher's wife had also told us about. Natural volcanic vents heat the sand around Kinko Bay, and a small service industry has grown up around turning the heated sand into an enjoyable bathing experience.

We paid an old woman a small fee to prepare our "bath." She carefully sifted the hot sand, creating the perfect temperature for a relaxing "soak." She gave us cotton *yukata* coverings to wear. While we put them on, she dug a hole, which she had us lie down in face-up. Then she covered us with hot sand from our feet to our necks. We stared across the beach, through palm trees waving in the wind, to the other side of the bay where we could see a smoking volcano. We felt we had found paradise. Donna crawled out of the sand and took goofy pictures of me looking like a mummy with my body covered in hot sand and my white head poking into the air.

We returned to Tokyo a week before Christmas. We had been in Japan a month. The leaves were gone, and the fastidious Japanese gardeners had carefully wrapped trees in muslin to protect them from the winter cold. Snow sprinkled the cheerfully decorated streets. As if on cue, people stopped dressing in fall mauves and donned winter blacks. We spent our last two weeks visiting museums, temples, shrines, art galleries, and amazing department stores which contained everything from restaurants to fantastic gardens. On Christmas Day we exchanged gifts and visited the Imperial Palace.

Just before we left Tokyo, on the 27th of December, I called Kazz to say goodbye. We didn't have much to say on the phone. He didn't ask about the five gods I still had remaining in San Francisco, nor had I brought them up during our stay. He wished us a safe trip home.

As our plane climbed, I recalled moments of clarity during the beautiful ceremony at Mount Katsuragi. The moving words of the teacher about world peace and the great love of Christ had been so direct and spoke to my heart. And yet, my doubts remained. Why were there so many secrets between Kazz, the teacher, and his followers? Were there more ominous things that they were hiding from me?

chapter 8

Donna put two feet forward while I put
only one.

*At the beginning of 1984, not long after I returned from
Japan, the famous doomsday clock of the Bulletin of the Atomic
Scientists was ominously moved ahead to three minutes before
midnight. The Bulletin, which has tracked international tension
and developments since 1947, said, "The blunt simplicities of
force threaten to displace any other form of discourse between the
superpowers."*

The sun was shining when we landed in San Francisco but I
hardly noticed. A few days later, at a New Year's Eve party
that Donna had quickly organized, I sat quietly in a corner,
feeling a darkness closing in around me. At midnight, while
the rest of the guests toasted 1984, Donna asked me what was

wrong. I offered the lame excuse of being tired, but she knew something more than jet lag had sapped my spirit.

Here I was back from a long visit to Japan, and I felt no closer to really understanding what I was caught up in than I did before I left. I had met Kazz and the teacher, and yet I felt I had only more questions. Furthermore, while Donna and I had traveled well together, six weeks of day-to-day intimacy had taken a toll on me. Now that we were back, I craved solitude. I needed time to sort out both the relationship and the Shinto project.

The year being welcomed by my champagne-sipping friends would prove to be one of the most difficult of my life. At first, I felt as though the world was simply against me and that I had no control over the outside forces that were making my life miserable. Only later, when things got better and I still felt miserable, did I began to suspect that I was contributing more to the problem than I had acknowledged.

Within days of returning from Japan, I contracted every bug that came within ten feet of me: colds, the flu, and finally pneumonia. The pneumonia put me on my back for two weeks, unable to move or work. Donna managed to avoid my harmful germs, but for the first time in her life, she developed violent allergic reactions to common things like dust, cats, and wool. It was the result, a doctor told her, of going from Japan's especially dry winter air to the dampness of San Francisco. Her incessant talk of moving to New York stopped, at least for a while.

In February, a month after I had recovered from pneumonia, Donna and I got in a terrifying car accident. We were headed home from an evening concert. I drove across the street at the exact moment the driver of a large white van full of late-night commuters was frantically pumping his failed brakes. He hit Donna's side of the car going full speed, tossing her onto my lap and pushing the car onto the sidewalk.

No one in the van was hurt, but Donna's back was injured, thankfully not seriously. My wrist was painfully sprained from trying to swerve the car to safety, and it would be a long time before I could hold anything, even a small camera. My right knee was swollen like a balloon from hitting the bottom of the dash. My car was totaled.

"Bad luck, eh?" I said as a friend drove us back home from the hospital. Then under my breath I said, "Or bad spirits."

"We were at the wrong place at the wrong time," Donna said.

"What's the difference?" I asked, and then neither of us spoke the rest of the way home.

Not long after the car accident, the death threats began. At first, I had no idea where they were coming from, or whom. I'd come home to my answering machine:

"You son of a bitch. You are dead."

The first time I figured it was a prank. But the threats continued, always with the same short threatening message.

We called the police: they authorized a call trace on my phone, but added that phone terror was becoming common. It was not, they said, to be taken too seriously.

It had been nearly a year since I wrote the newspaper article on the Shinto project, but in the meantime, with Kazz's reluctant approval, I had given permission to *Not Man Apart*, a national ecology magazine, and *East West Journal* to reprint the story. I was now getting responses from all over the country.

"Your article doesn't have anything to do with the threats," Donna said one day. I told her I agreed: after all, the responses to the reprints were all positive. People wanted to help.

Nonetheless, after Donna left and I was sitting at my desk alone, I felt fear spread through my body like a fever. My chest, still tight from the pneumonia, felt as though it would burst. I played the latest message from my machine, desperately listening for a clue to the caller's identity. My heart began pounding furiously, out of control, and then seemed to move like vomit up my throat. Could the caller be some crazed survivor of Pearl Harbor with a lifetime vendetta against the Japanese? Was it some right-wing religious nut, embarking on a holy war against the infidels, against pagans? In near panic I stared at the gods left on my bookshelf. In my mind I reassembled all the pieces of the Sword of Heaven to make a single shiny steel blade. Strangely, the mere thought of the powerful weapon gave me courage, and I felt protected from the angry voice on the tape.

It didn't take long for me to go deeply into debt. I was charging everything, even my rent. The bills from hotels, restaurants, and camera stores in Japan arrived. Even though Donna offered to help me financially, I refused. I felt we had settled into a comfortable rhythm, splitting our time between her place and mine, and I didn't want to upset the delicate balance between being close and being too close that would come with financial strings. At least that is how I understood it at the time.

At first it was easy to blame my six weeks away, the illness, and the accident for my financial woes. But when the situation didn't get better, I could only blame myself. Instead of hustling work, as I should have, I spent long hours in the library, reading, researching, and contemplating the nature of Shinto.

I wasn't interested in converting. I wasn't writing a theological or philosophical dissertation. But I did hunger to understand the religion at the base of the project in which I now, for better or worse, was a player.

On the surface it seemed so simple: Shinto was the worship of nature and the ancestors. But what did it mean to worship nature: to call a stone or a tree a god? And why did it seem that Shinto and the fanatic worship of the emperor were never far apart? Was there an inherent flaw in Shinto that actually encouraged a fanatical approach to the world, rather than the sensible moderation espoused by other Eastern religions such as Buddhism?

The first book I consulted was Gerald L. Berry's *Religions of the World*, published in 1947, not long after the end of World War II. Berry was downright disdainful: "The best that can be said of Shinto is that there were never bloody sacrifices or cruel or immoral rituals. It has no appeal to any instinct of good or evil; and it is hollow and empty, promising no definite destiny. What its future will be since Emperor Hirohito has renounced his claim to divinity is uncertain."

The great Buddhist philosopher, Suzuki, who is commonly credited with bringing Zen Buddhism to the Western world, seemed at best ambivalent about Shinto. Writing about the Shinto sword in his book *Zen and Japan,* Suzuki said: "[The sword] betrays [Shinto's] naturalistic origin. It is not a symbol but an object endowed with some mysterious power. Here lingers an animistic way of thinking...Shintoism has no philosophy of its own to stand on; it is awakened to its own consciousness and existence only when it comes in contact with one of the others, and thereby learns how to express itself."

I found corroboration for my friend's earlier remark that Shinto was outlawed in the U.S. during World War II.

Prejudice, War and the Constitution stated that religious services could be performed by Japanese-American Protestants, Catholics, and Buddhists during the war, but Shinto ceremonies were forbidden.

I found pictures of the Shinto shrine, which stood inside Golden Gate Park, taken before it was torn down during the war. It had been a medium-sized pavilion, with a high, slanted roof and beautifully carved patterns in the wood beams. I couldn't see from the photograph what was inside, but the shrine fit so nicely into its park surroundings that I felt shocked that they had actually leveled it.

Did government officials know something I didn't? Was the practice of Shinto really that threatening?

Finally I found some books that were more helpful. Joseph Campbell's *Oriental Mythology* contains an amusing anecdote. A Western sociologist was frustrated in his long attempt to understand the ideology and theology of Shinto. He expressed his frustration to a Shinto priest, who smiled as he said to the scholar, "We do not have ideology. We do not have theology. We dance." Campbell then adds, "Which, precisely, is the point. For Shinto, at its root, is a religion not of sermons but of awe: which is a sentiment that may or may not produce words, but in either case goes beyond them."

Campbell, in the same book, also spoke of "astonishing affinities" between Shinto mythology and those of other northern cultures, such as the Irish, Siberians, and natives of the Canadian Northeast. I remembered the ease with which my father and other Norwegians as well as Native Americans seemed to accept the story of the Shinto gods.

It was both reassuring and disconcerting to read from *Shinto, The Kami Way* that "except for the student [with] almost inexhaustible resources and time for his investigation, Shinto remains practically a closed book. There are very few people, Japanese or foreign, who understand Shinto thoroughly and are able to explain it in detail."

"Even the Japanese don't know," I thought with some satisfaction.

One of the best books that I found was *The Looking-Glass God* by Nahum Stiskin. The book gives detailed explanations of every aspect of Shinto rites and rituals and draws well-thought-out parallels between Eastern mysticism and Western science. "Shinto is not a religion in the normal sense of the word.... Of course, if an awareness of the invisible energies of life, an awe before the immensity of the cosmos, a deep humility with regard to the smallness of oneself, and a never-ending gratitude for the order within nature are taken to be defining characteristics of religion, then Shinto is indeed one.... What then, is Shinto? In the final analysis, it is a pure expression of human intuition...[which] is the universal inheritance of mankind and is the root of human existence."

This made sense to me, and appealed to my rational Western mind fostered by my father. It also spoke to what I indeed feel are some of the essential elements of spirituality. And interestingly, it had been my intuition which had gotten me involved in the first place.

I also began taking Japanese language lessons. The beginning classes, offered by the Japanese Society of Northern California, met twice a week for three months. We mostly learned simple survival phrases such as "Hello," "Good morning," "Where are you from?" "How much is it?" and the like. But we also learned some of the basics of Japanese writing: *hiragana*, a phonetic script not unlike Roman letters; *katakana*, another phonetic script used solely for Japanese words; and *kanji*, the visual script inherited from the Chinese which contains both a pictorial and literal meaning. There are more than 3,000 *kanji* symbols, and even the most literate Japanese cannot know them all.

"This helps…it all helps," I told Donna after explaining to her how *kanji* characters were both pictures and words at the same time.

I explained how our Japanese language teacher had told us that the brain of people who study Japanese from an early age physically develops differently because they are exercising both the literal and the figurative capabilities at once. The right side of the brain, which handles mostly visual information, and which is also considered the side most responsible for intuitive insight, is actually more developed in the Japanese than in people who learn only a Western language. As a result the Japanese generally put more emphasis on nonrational or intuitive approaches to problem solving.

"Like artists!" exclaimed Donna.

"She also said that in Western languages there is a sharp distinction between subject and object: I, you, it. In Japan, "I" or "you" is rarely used. They are assumed."

"No wonder we were confused when we were there," Donna said.

"My teacher told the class that the Japanese are more interested in harmony and consideration for one another's feelings. They prefer suggesting things and hinting, or indirect reference, so they can change direction without hurting anyone's feelings. We saw that too, didn't we?"

"Yes!"

"One last thing. She told us that they don't use the Greek logic of precision, where something is either/or. In the West, we always want something to be good or bad, hot or cold, odd or even, this or that. If something is in between, we call it ambiguous which carries a negative connotation. In Japanese there is a special word for the third alternative, *mu*, which carries as much importance as either/or."

"I'm not sure I understand," Donna said.

"Me either," I confessed.

"Are you trying too hard? I mean, I like the stuff you're saying. But don't you think you are getting a little too philosophical? Too much in your head? Aren't you overdoing all this research?"

"I know, I know," I replied. I appreciated Donna's support, and I knew she was right that I was tying too hard. But as I saw it, Kazz was less than forthcoming, and books and Japanese classes offered an important way into Shinto and the project. I felt incapable of sitting still and letting understanding come slowly with time.

Even though I hadn't tried to place a god in more than six months, the Shinto project continued both from San Francisco and Japan. Too confused and too broke to place gods myself, I continued sending them with friends to other parts of the world. Helen Johnston, owner of the Focus Gallery in San Francisco, took one to Kenya and put it in Lake Naivasha. "The Shinto god was dropped about 6 p.m. My great worry is that the lake with the current drought may shrink enough to expose it. It was down when I was there for I had to cross a muddy area to reach the lake's edge. Well, we can only hope!"

Michael Winn, a writer friend of Juan Li's, took one to the Kun Lung mountains, a restricted area of China where the Chinese military perform nuclear tests.

Barbara Schneider, a Bay Area woman who had responded to the *California Living* article, carried a Shinto god to Egypt and placed it in the Nile River, near the temple of Karnak.

My good friend Barry Marshall, a land surveyor, took one to Morocco and placed it in a shallow lake near Azorou.

He wrote a beautiful letter about the placing. He ended with: "A little faith and a stone tossed in a lake may make a world of difference or none at all…it is harmless. And ripples are magic.…"

"Harmless," I thought to myself as I reread his letter. "Yeah, harmless…as long as you aren't too involved."

Kazz, too, was busy. He wrote and told me about placing gods in the Middle East, China, and North Korea. He was traveling at amazing speed, crisscrossing the earth as if it were just a few miles wide. One month I received a letter from Israel, where he placed a god in the Sinai desert. Then I heard he had just returned from a grueling trip to Karachi, Islamabad, and Bombay. He finished the trip by traveling through Nepal and Tibet to climb and place a god on holy Mount Kailas.

Borders seemed to open magically for him. I was astonished that he was able to enter Iran, carrying not one but several of the stone encased gods. When the border guards asked him what they were, he told them "Gods from Japan," and they hastily put them back in the bag and hurried him through. "They are so fanatic," Kazz said, "that the mention of God scared them."

But not all was right with him either. His wife, fed up with all his travels, left home with their daughters for three months. His back, which had been better, was again giving him serious trouble after the strenuous trips.

"Her mother convinced her to leave," Kazz wrote, "and now she isn't talking to me." He blamed the separation on "bad spirits."

Donna and I weren't getting along either. The tension exploded just after my 32nd birthday in June. On the surface, the issue was vacation. She wanted to make plans to go somewhere, anywhere. I made excuse after excuse for not being able to commit: no money, no time, too much work. But the issue wasn't vacation, or money, or time, and Donna knew it. Her brown eyes flashed and her hands went to her hips.

"You can't make up your mind about anything! About me. About the Shinto project."

I started to protest, but then stopped.

"What do you *want*?" she asked.

"I don't understand."

"I can never tell for sure what you want. You're so vague."

She went to a drawer and pulled out a print I had made for her. A few weeks earlier, we had taken a stroll on the beach where Donna combed the sand for driftwood and rocks that she could incorporate into her drawings. Inspired by her very personal art, I focused my camera on nature, a clear departure from my normal journalistic and documentary work. I had taken a picture of our feet, Donna's boots and my white tennis shoe.

"See," she said, "My two feet are here, but you, you have only one foot forward. It's what you always do: put just one foot forward. I'm really tired of it. Jump, for god's sake. Be bold!"

"There are other shots with both my feet showing."

"Then it's strange that you chose this shot to print," she said, leaning against the wall. "It was your choice."

The next morning at breakfast Donna handed me a piece of paper with a Kahil Gibran poem she had carefully transcribed. I read it and put it away without comment even though I was profoundly moved by its wisdom.

> Doubt is a pain
> too lonely to know
> that faith
> is his twin brother

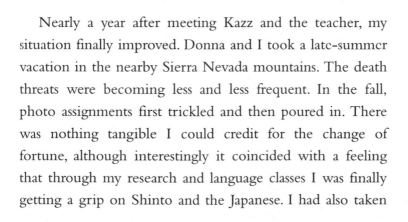

Nearly a year after meeting Kazz and the teacher, my situation finally improved. Donna and I took a late-summer vacation in the nearby Sierra Nevada mountains. The death threats were becoming less and less frequent. In the fall, photo assignments first trickled and then poured in. There was nothing tangible I could credit for the change of fortune, although interestingly it coincided with a feeling that through my research and language classes I was finally getting a grip on Shinto and the Japanese. I had also taken

Donna's comments to heart and was trying to be more engaged in the relationship.

As 1984 closed, I suggested a fancy restaurant to celebrate.
We toasted the year of bad luck, laughing bravely at the
memories of the car accident, our illnesses, the death threats
and our fights. I was filled with confidence that the dark
cloud had passed.

Not long after, I suggested that we take a week off to visit
Donna's father in Florida. He'd taken a winter house in
Venice, on the Gulf, and since he was divorced and alone,
there was plenty of room for us. The vacation would cost us
only airfare. Suddenly, I remembered that none of the
Shinto gods had been placed in that part of the world.
Although I had sent seven gods to faraway places, I had not
personally placed any gods since the first in Norway a year
and a half earlier.

The whole year I was soul searching, the world hadn't
gotten any safer. The confrontation between the two superpowers, which had escalated in the early 1980s, was more
intense than ever. Star Wars, instead of diffusing a stressful
situation, actually made things worse. Many Americans,
including me, didn't believe the plan would work and
thought Star Wars was instead a tremendous waste of time
and money. The Soviets considered it a further arms buildup
and feared that it was a prelude to a nuclear attack. Nuclear
trauma still gripped the world.

Perhaps this was the time for me to place another god.

Within moments of deciding to take a god, a storm of doubt hit me. "What am I doing? Another god?" I made a silent prayer to no one in particular. "Please make this easy, not confusing like the Lab or Shasta. I want to help, I truly do."

chapter 9

The newspaper headline says it all.

"You have certainly heard of the 'butterfly effect.' The belief that everything in the world is so mysteriously and comprehensively interconnected that a slight, seemingly insignificant wave of a butterfly's wing in a single spot on this planet can unleash a typhoon thousands of miles away."

—Czechoslovak poet and Cold War dissident Vaclav Havel

It started so normally. Donna's father, Don Speed, picked us up at the St. Petersburg airport and drove us the 60 miles south to Venice. Within an hour we had changed into our swimsuits and were strolling on the nearby beach, our white skin turning pink in the intense sun. Don, a retired Air Force captain whom I liked immediately, walked with us fully clothed, happy to be with younger company.

"I call them AIAs," he explained, pointing disdainfully at a group of retirees, their heads bent between their knees, buckets filled with shells that they had stooped to collect. "Asses in the Air."

"But Dad, I saw a bucket of shells at the house!" Donna teased. "Don't talk."

"Those weren't shells. They're fossilized shark teeth, a million years old. Find one this size," he said, pointing to the palm of his hand, "and you fetch a hundred bucks. This beach is one of the few places in the world where they exist."

Five days passed quickly. The weather was perfect and one day blurred into the next. The soft air and gentle breezes made it easy for Donna and me to relax and enjoy each other.

We snorkeled, sunbathed, and collected sharks' teeth. I found one the size of my fist, but it was broken, and Don said it was only a good souvenir with little monetary value. In the evening we watched TV or played poker, using the teeth as money.

During these games, I encouraged Don to tell me more about his life. I learned that he was underage when he enlisted during World War II, and he had to get his mother's written permission before the military would accept him. He chose to fly because he didn't want to walk, and he became a navigator aboard the B-52 bomber. When he had finished his required missions, mostly over Italy, he signed up for more.

"Donald Wilbur Speed. Mr. John Wayne, flyboy!" teased Donna who had long ago stopped calling her dad sir.

Following the war he moved to California with his new wife and young son. Donna was born soon after, in the Central Valley town of Fresno. When she was just an infant, her family moved to urban San Francisco where Don took a job selling business machines.

"Why couldn't I have been born in San Francisco and not Fresno? It'd look so much better on my résumé!" Donna joked.

Then came the Korean War, and Don was recalled by the Air Force and back into the familiar cockpit of the B-52 bomber. When that war was over he decided to make the Air Force and B-52s his life.

"I have a picture of me and my brother taken when I was three or four, with Santa Claus," giggled Donna. "We are both wearing sweatshirts with B-52s on them!"

Although Don offered to drive us to different beaches, we preferred the beach near his house. Looking for the teeth there made each day a treasure hunt.

In the evenings, Donna spread the day's treasures out on a white piece of paper and sketched them. I marveled at her ability to turn common shells into things of magic and beauty. But art was her life. It was her work and her play. It was her way of defining the world, as well as her way of communicating with it. I envied the clarity she found in her art.

One day as I leaned over to look closer at a drawing, I caught her scent. Its freshness made me dizzy. The daily sun had bronzed her hair, turning it more red than brown. She seemed to glow.

"I'm really glad we're here," I whispered. My ambivalence about our relationship was gone, at least for the moment.

She turned and smiled at me, and then went back to her sketching.

On Wednesday I called the airline to confirm our Saturday flight back. Don didn't have a phone, so I walked five blocks to a nearby shopping mall. When I reached the airline, I learned that Donna's ticket was set for Saturday but on mine the agent had mistakenly written Thursday, tomorrow. It was a non-refundable, restricted ticket, and there was no way to change it without a huge penalty. I was heartbroken that the great vacation and my time with Donna would be cut short. The only good news came when I checked in with my answering machine. Two photography jobs for next week, a message from my friend Perry about a possible trip to the Philippines, and, to my relief, no death threats.

Thursday morning was clear, with just a few cumulus clouds to the south. They passed and left a hazy sky. Donna and I took our now customary early morning walk on the beach. I carried snorkeling equipment, and Donna carried a big bag with our towels, suntan lotion, and the Shinto god.

"I won't be long, " I said, squinting to stare across the Gulf.

"Your plane leaves in three hours."

I slipped on my heavy black flippers, then wiped sand from my mask and snorkel. Donna handed me the *kami,* and I removed the white cloth, exposing the Japanese prayer paper covering the stone god.

"Be careful of the speedboats."

"Be careful, be careful," I replied teasingly. "Of course I'll be careful." I hugged her, drawing her small body against me and kissing her. My back was to the rising sun, hers to the Gulf.

"It's not too heavy?" she asked as we parted.

"No, I can manage."

I stepped awkwardly into the cool water. An elderly couple walked by. Their heads were dropped to the sand, AIAs, looking intently for fossilized sharks' teeth.

As I flapped away from shore using only one arm I thought, This thing *is* heavy. A motorboat sped by, then a sleek sailboat. I switched the god from one hand to the other, experimenting with different strokes. Keeping my face downward, I watched as the bottom changed from sand to corral, then back to sand. I paused to rest about 1,000 yards out and noticed an empty crab trap resting on the bottom.

Glancing over my shoulder, I saw that Donna was a speck

on the horizon, part of the sandy beach. My confidence waned as I realized how far out I was into the cold water. Three large fish darted under me. I let both my arms drag behind me, propelling myself with only my flippers.

Wap, wap. I jerked my head up. The noise, which sounded like hands clapping, stopped as I did. I swam, and the sound resumed. *Wap, wap.* I stopped. It can't be…. My skin erupted into a mass of goose bumps. Come on, don't be ridiculous, that's only in the movies…but if it is real, I could use this stone, this god…and smash the hell out of…whatever it is. I started swimming again.

Wap, wap. Damn this stone…It's really slowing me down. It's heavy. I could swim so much faster without it. I gripped it tighter. The paper wrapping disintegrated, exposing a granite-like stone.

Wap, wap. I turned my head to watch. *Wap, wap.* Jesus, how stupid. The sound was my fins hitting the surface. I was afraid of my own shadow.

At a second crab trap, a mile out, I stopped. Boats sped by dangerously close. For a moment, I thought about simply dropping the god and returning to shallow water. But I'd come too far not to do it right. I dove. At 15 feet my ears popped; I stopped for a moment, held my nose, and blew carefully, freeing the pressure so I could continue deeper. At 25 feet I hit bottom. The sand was compacted, so I pressed hard, embedding the god. It wasn't covered, but it was secure. I shot to the surface, gasping for air.

Once in warmer water, I dove for sharks' teeth, but I didn't find any large ones.

Now I could see Donna clearly. She was lying on the beach, reading a book. When she saw me she jumped up and waved.

"Why did you have to go out so far?" she asked when I sloshed up on the shore. "I couldn't see you. I took lots of pictures, but then you disappeared."

"Just scared the hell out of myself. I thought I heard a shark, but it was just my flippers. Guess I was a little tense. But then I thought to myself: I did it! I placed another god. Whatever barrier prevented me from placing a god at the Lab and on top of Mount Shasta was gone. This isn't so bad after all.

Flying home was uneventful. I wrote in my diary how perfect everything had been except for the mix-up with the plane ticket. I liked the idea of the broken Shinto sword, lying with the destructive but now harmless and beautiful shark teeth. When I got home, after stopovers in St. Louis and Denver, I went straight to bed and a dreamless sleep.

The sound of the phone jerked me awake. It was Donna, and her voice was anxious. I looked at the clock. It was past eleven in the morning my time, and past two in the afternoon in Florida.

"You won't believe what happened!"

"Your Dad…"

"No, he's okay."

"Then what?" I asked.

"A tornado…"

She paused to calm herself.

"…A tornado just missed our house!"

I whistled.

"Where did it start?" I asked.

"At seven this morning. The noise was awful."

"No, where?"

"You're not going to believe this," she answered. "There's a map in the afternoon paper. It started…it started almost exactly where you placed the god."

"Off the beach?"

"Yeah, directly off the beach. On the approach to the small airport."

"How far out?"

"A mile or so. Really, it was right where you placed the god."

I was speechless.

"We just returned from downtown. Incredible destruction. Entire buildings disappeared. And there is worse news."

"What?" I asked incredulously.

"Two people died."

I suddenly felt very cold. It was my fault, of course. I had placed the god and provoked bad spirits. But wasn't it then *not* my fault? Clearly it was the fault of the bad spirits. But then again, since I didn't believe in spirits, I couldn't very well blame it on them.

In the silence I gripped the receiver even tighter. It had to be my fault. The storm was a manifestation of my own confusion about the project and my inner turmoil about life. The same thing had happened on Mount Shasta with the storm and my friend getting altitude sickness. But at least on Mount Shasta, during the storm, no one was killed.

Donna's voice brought me back to reality.

"Are you there? Are you okay?"

This is crazy, I thought as I mumbled something back to her. What am I thinking? My fault? Bad spirits? It's just another coincidence. An unlucky meeting of time and event. Nothing more, nothing less. My god, I'm starting to lose my sense of reality. I'm going crazy.

Finally Donna said, "I've got to go. Don is waiting."

Before we hung up I asked her to do me a favor.

"Go to the beach and see if the god washed up. Will you do that?"

That evening she called. There was rubble everywhere, she said, crab traps strewn all over the beach. But there was no Shinto god.

I tried to put the incident out of my mind, and finally, after an hour of tossing and turning fitfully, I fell asleep.

A little while later, I dreamed I was in the bomb shelter and Kazz was on the phone. I told him about the tornado and the god, and he was excited. I felt an intense feeling of affection toward him and my eyes filled with tears. After a few moments of silence, Kazz hung up, but even after the phone connection was broken I felt his presence. Then I turned from the phone, looked down, and saw a huge, slimy footprint. I noticed the back door was open. An awful shadow passed and I screamed.

The nightmare jerked me awake. It took me a long time to go back to sleep.

chapter 10

On a native *vinta* in southern Philippines
just before the placing.

*In 1985, Ronald Reagan was sworn in as president for a second
term and Mikhail Gorbachev became the leader of the USSR.
The mass antinuclear demonstrations of earlier years had failed to
stop the deployment of tactical missiles in Europe and now anti-
war activists turned their full attention to another arena of the
Cold War—the proxy war in Central America. In January,
Daniel Ortega was sworn in as Nicaragua's first democratically
elected president. President Reagan called Ortega a "tin-pot
dictator" and continued his support of the anti-government group
called the Contras whom Reagan called "the moral equivalent of
the Founding Fathers." The Soviets supplied the Nicaraguan
government with MIG fighters and MI-25 attack helicopters. As
the superpowers watched safely from afar, the Cold War turned hot
and real people died real deaths.*

Not long after returning from Florida, I received a call from the public relations agency my friend Perry had called about, asking if I wanted to join a group of travel writers and photographers on a trip to the Philippines. The "junket" was scheduled to leave on June 3, 1985, my 33rd birthday. I wavered. Dictator Ferdinand Marcos's control of the tattered Southeast Asian island nation was collapsing, making the chances of selling a travel story about the country slim. But then as an afterthought the PR man told me that the flight stopped in Tokyo on the way back and I could lay over if I wanted. Quickly I accepted the invitation. Not only was there a chance to place another god, but I could ask the teacher in Japan about the tornado.

It turned out that the travel junket left very little room for spontaneity or individual deviation. The Philippine travel association had scheduled every minute of our time. After an eighteen-hour flight to the Philippines, we were to rest for a few days in Manila and then fly to the southern island of Mindanao, then to Cebu on the east coast, and finally to Baguio in the north on the island of Luzon. We would always be accompanied by local guides.

The 7,000-plus tropical islands that make up the Philippines have all the ingredients needed for a conventional travel story: beautiful beaches, fantastic swimming and diving, and breathtaking landscapes. But from the moment we arrived, I found myself fascinated by things other than recreation. Few places in the world have seen as much drama as the Philippines, due in part to its strategic military significance. One of the first "tourist" spots we visited was the cemetery for 38,000 Americans who died in fierce fighting with the Japanese in World War II. We later flew over Subic Bay, at the time the major American military base for the entire South Pacific. The bay was a key U.S. outpost during the Cold War, and a supply base for American military adventures in Vietnam and even the Middle East.

And as if the country's critical geopolitical position weren't enough, the islands are subject to some of the worst disasters in the world. Earthquakes, hurricanes, and typhoons destroy huge parts of the country with awesome regularity. Cultural and political storms, meanwhile, raged between the Muslims and Christians, as well as between the communists and the government. The sum total made the Philippines a rather adventurous place to vacation.

By the fourth day of our hectic schedule, while our plane circled Zamboanga City in the southern Philippines, I had accepted the reality that the Shinto god I carried in my camera bag might still be with me when I landed in Tokyo.

Looking out my window, I noticed two distinct islands not far from the busy city. "Those are the Santa Cruz islands," said one of the Philippine guides in answer to my question. "Look, one is shaped like a heart, the other like a dagger."

"A dagger? Where?" I asked before I noticed the slender strip of land adjacent to a round island covered in green. The dagger was there, but it took an active imagination to turn the other island into a heart.

"There is a legend, told by sea gypsies, which explains the origin of the Santa Cruz Islands," my guide continued. "It's about a Muslim girl and her pagan lover who were not allowed to marry because of their differences. One night, under the cover of a storm, the boy fetched the girl in a fishing boat. She was terrified of the wrath of her parents and her God Allah, but the boy, reaching into his belt and pulling out a dagger, assured her she was safe from both. When the young couple was discovered missing, people from both tribes searched all night, but the storm became so violent that they had to stop. In the morning all they found were two islands where before there were none: a heart and dagger, forever separated by a deep channel of water.

"Sad, eh?" he concluded.

That night, at an outdoor restaurant overlooking the harbor, we feasted on giant lobster, grilled fish, and roasted pork. Beyond our terrace we could see the equatorial sun quickly dropping behind the Santa Cruz Islands. The sky went from a deep azure to pink to black.

"No one is allergic to lobster?" a guide asked. "We had quite a problem with the last group."

"I've never seen such a big lobster. It could feed a small town!" said one of the travel writers.

"Tomorrow," the guide said, "we'll board native *vintas* (outrigger-fitted canoes) and paddle to the larger of the islands, the dagger. The heart is used by the military and is off-limits."

"What about the missing Japanese tourists?" asked one of our group, a newspaper reporter whose slurred voice suggested too much San Miguel beer.

"Ah, you remember that?" the guide said hesitantly. "An unfortunate incident. Don't worry. The island is safe now. We'll have a picnic. There is…"

"What tourists?" I interrupted.

"Didn't you know?" the newspaper man said. "A year or so ago, a few Muslims kidnapped two Japanese tourists as a kind of joke. Things really got out of hand. They panicked and turned them over to the communist rebels. It's reported that the Japanese government paid a million dollars ransom. Maybe that's why you don't see any Japanese tourists," he said, laughing while he motioned with his hand around the restaurant.

Actually he was wrong. There *were* Japanese tourists. We had seen them strolling earlier by the pool, powerful-looking men with nearly every inch of their bodies covered with tattoos. They had young attractive women with them. It didn't take much of an imagination to figure out that these were *Yakuzi,* members of the dreaded Japanese Mafia, on vacation. These people—yet another shadow of modern Japan—were not going to be messed with by anyone.

"Just what I need for my travel story," I muttered. "More danger."

I learned something else that evening. I *am* allergic to equatorial lobster. In the middle of the night, I woke up with my entire body on fire, feeling as if tiny needles were pricking me. My head ached. I was awake, yet delirious. In my altered state, I recalled the story of the Santa Cruz Islands. I imagined the island shaped like a dagger thrust deeply into the one shaped like a heart. Pouring out of the gaping wound, along with blood and filth, came a horde of Japanese tourists, with cameras dangling from their shoulders. I dragged myself to the bathroom and threw up.

The next day, when I stepped onto the *vinta* that would take us the short distance to the islands, I felt better. The cool sea air eased my pain, although my skin still felt thin, nearly transparent. The dagger-shaped island was tranquil. Large palm and talisay trees reached across a pristine beach, and bougainvillea bloomed as red and intense as the equatorial sun. While the others picnicked under the shade of the broad-leafed talisay trees, I wandered over to one of the young boys who had ferried us to the island. I decided after the legend and my bizarre dream the night before that the god would go here, in water between the heart and the dagger. With the strict schedule of the junket, I didn't know if I'd have another chance.

"Do you speak English?" I asked the boy.

"Yes, a little. I live on the tip of the island and go to school in town."

"What's your name?"

"Alwadi," he said, smiling easily.

He must have been only eleven or twelve years old, but he acted much older, as children often do in Third World countries.

I asked him about the kidnapped Japanese tourists, thinking it would give us something to talk about other than the usual.

"Sure, everyone knows about that."

"Do you know the people who did it?" I asked, prodding him, thinking he might like to brag.

He shrugged and shook his head.

"Why did they do it?"

"My father used to tell me stories about the Japanese during the war when they occupied the island. They weren't

very nice. He was very happy when the Americans liber-
ated us."

I made up some story about wanting to dive for shells.
Then I asked if he would take me to the middle of the
channel in his boat.

"It's very deep. The current is strong," he cautioned.

"Five dollars," I said, knowing it was a fortune to him.

He waved me toward his boat.

In the middle of the channel as our boat swayed and
tossed in the strong current, I unwrapped the cloth that
covered the Japanese stone god. I looked at Alwadi and was
surprised to see fear on his face. He had quickly figured out
that I wasn't interested in diving for shells. But why was he
scared? His face begged for an explanation.

I said, without much thought, "It's a memorial. I'm
doing it for a Japanese friend. His father was killed here
during the war."

He didn't believe me, and his look of fear turned into a
look of terror. I could have been holding a bomb and gotten
the same effect.

Maybe I should have just told him the truth. Instead, as I
hesitated, I launched into a farcical imaginary dialogue.
Alwadi, this is a Japanese god. Yes, this stone that I'm holding.
Surely you believe in such things as stone gods. It's called the
Sword of Heaven and supposedly a piece of an ancient sword
is embedded inside. A broken sword. But don't get me

wrong. It may be broken but it's powerful. How powerful? You should have seen what happened in Florida! Anyway, I'll place it in the water—right here between the islands, the islands your people call the dagger and the heart.

Do you get the symbolism? Dagger and heart? You do? Oh, good.

But there's more. This will bring peace to your land. It will end war. Maybe it will even rid you of your dictator Marcos. You'd like that, right?

Yes, I know, the god is from Japan. I understand, that might be a problem. But the Japanese are human too, you know. They make mistakes. They're sorry for what happened during World War II. At least, the ones that I know are.

Me? A Japan apologist? No, no. I'm just a photo-journalist, following a story. Okay, I admit, I've stepped over the line. Not much detachment or objectivity here. Guess I'm human too.

Alwadi's eyes remained locked on mine as I continued my unspoken monologue. The fear in his eyes cut through to my core being.

Your face! Please don't look that way. Please don't be afraid. I won't hurt you. You're too young to be scared. It's not good for you. Fear is insidious. It'll numb you. It'll keep you from fully enjoying life, from participating in it. You won't be able to make decisions. It'll keep you from loving. You'll never absorb the good when you are filled with fear. Don't be afraid of me. Don't be afraid of anything. It'll screw you up.

My internal remarks continued, full of guilt and confusion as well as truth. It felt like an eternity, but it was only a few moments. My final thought before I tossed the stone overboard was that the project had now driven me completely crazy. I said sharply, "Let's go."

Alwadi didn't speak to me again. But later I saw him talking to a group of elderly men and pointing at me. The easy smiles were gone. I had no idea what Alwadi told them or what they were thinking. I only knew I wanted to get off the island as quickly as possible. How was it that I ended up spreading fear when I wanted to foster peace? I wondered whether the problem was inherent in the project, or rather might not lie within me. Perhaps I could find some answers in Japan.

chapter 11

At the teacher's house in Osaka.

*"Hiroshima did not die. The waters of the Ohta River flowed
clearly through its seven channels. The pure and limpid water was
very beautiful. I wanted to become that water, because water knows
neither pain nor sorrow. The clear stream of the Ohta washed away
the suffering from my heart. By letting my heart merge with the
water, I have been able to feel some of the happiness I felt before."*

—Hiromi Sakaguchi, a 5th grade student who lost his parents
and four siblings to the atomic bomb

It was a four-hour flight from Manila to Tokyo and then a
two-hour bus ride from Narita airport to the Asia Center
Hotel downtown where Donna and I had stayed a year and
a half earlier. It was raining and cold, quite a contrast from
the torrid weather of Manila. "You are lucky," Kazz said on

the 13th of June when I called. "We are having a private ceremony at the teacher's house on Saturday night. Please come and visit. It will be very different from the last ceremony you saw."

Since it was only Thursday, that meant I had all day Friday in Tokyo. I would use the day to see what I could find out about Kazz and his group.

The man at the Tokyo press information office was busy but intrigued by my question.

"Not too many foreigners are interested in Shinto," he said. He motioned me to the back of the room. "Let's try the library and see what we can find in English."

"Frankly speaking," he said after we found translations of a government-sponsored religious survey, "young people like myself aren't very interested in Shinto either."

"Here," I cried, pointing to an official government report. "This is the group I was telling you about. Tenkokyo, located in the Yamaguchi prefecture."

"There are more than 145 Shinto groups," observed the press officer. We both read that Kazz's group was considered one of the traditional sects of Shinto (*kyoha* Shinto), but that only meant it was founded between 1868 and 1945. The categories were based on chronology rather than doctrine. There was also Shrine Shinto (*jinja* Shinto), which came into existence prior to the modern era, and New Sect Shinto (*shinkyoha* Shinto), covering postwar groups.

Shinto, according to these reports, provided fertile ground

for a wide variety of ritual and myth. Some of the sects were founded simply on the vision of one person, who received inspiration either directly from a *kami* or from devoting his or her life to strict religious training and practice. During the sixteenth century, a man named Hasegawa Kakugyo espoused climbing Mount Fuji as a religious act and inspired the Fusokyo sect, which even today is active in organizing religious expeditions up Mount Fuji.

Hirayama Shosai, a nineteenth century government magistrate, believed that purification came from ascetic exercises such as standing under a cold waterfall. Based on these beliefs, he founded a popular sect known as Taiseikyo.

Many of the holy Shinto leaders were women such as Deguchi Nao (1836–1918), the founder of the Omoto sect, whose divine revelation called for nothing less than the reconstruction of the world and the creation of an ideal society.

Persecution of sects by the government was rare, but it happened. Onishi Aijiro, for example, was a charismatic Shinto leader at the turn of this century who quickly received the wrath of the government when he denied the emperor's divinity. Japan, he wrote, was on its way to another world war and annihilation. Along with a thousand of his followers—mostly military officers—he was arrested, tried, and jailed for his radical ideas.

"There are also over 80,000 registered Shinto shrines in Japan," I read aloud from another report. In Japan, any thing or any place can become a shrine: a single tree or an entire village or an entire mountain are preserved as long as they have a *kami* nature. A simple rice straw rope wrapped around a stone or a tree may be the only marker needed to show that an object is sacred and the dwelling of a *kami*.

The most important Shinto site is the Ise Jingu Shrines, part of which is dedicated to the Sun Goddess herself. It has been a sacred site for more than 1,300 years and remarkably, is rebuilt every 20 years regardless of its condition with no change whatsoever in design or construction materials. The next rebuilding was scheduled for 1993 and again in 2013.

"It doesn't say much more about Tenkokyo, the group you are interested in," said the officer. "What's so special about it?"

"That's what I'm here to find out."

In truth, my visit to the press information office comforted me. So much of the project was surrounded by mystery. The fact that the group was officially recognized gave me something concrete to grab onto, and I was at least thankful for that.

On Saturday, Kazz and I embraced at the Osaka train station. Despite our frequent misunderstandings, I felt we were actually becoming friends. Our ongoing communication helped, but I think deep down we both accepted the ideas that fate had brought us together and that we were participants in something much larger than either of us.

We drove in silence from the Osaka train station through the late-afternoon traffic to the teacher's suburban house. After our first meeting a year and a half earlier, I knew better than to barrage him with questions, and somehow I also felt more comfortable in the silence.

This time, though, it was the teacher who was interested in what I said. After politely asking me about Donna and my trip to the Philippines (he was only mildly curious about the placing there), he asked about Florida. I had written Kazz about the placing, and sent him the newspaper clippings of the tornado, but the teacher wanted me to repeat all the details. He listened intently while I recounted the story of the shark teeth, the mix-up with my ticket, and the tornado. But before I could ask him what he thought of the deaths of two people, he showed us to a room in the back and excused himself. He had to prepare for the ceremony. His wife and a housekeeper entered and brought us tea and melon.

When the teacher returned a while later, I tried to talk with him, but other people were filling the room, and the teacher turned his attention to them. Soon, there were about twenty people in the small tatami mat room in the back, greeting one another enthusiastically. They discreetly removed their street clothes and donned white robes. The teacher's wife and helper served tea and light snacks. Kazz was busy talking in Japanese to the others, so I moved back to the wall, watching and listening.

The teacher left again for a few moments, and this time returned dressed in a simple white robe. He waved us to a room off the front room, which housed a shrine much like the one I had seen on my first trip to Mount Katsuragi, only smaller. It was recessed from the main room on a stagelike platform. Hanging over the miniature wood temple was a straw rope with short strips of paper folded into zigzag patterns. At the base of the temple were offerings of rice, water, and salt on wooden stands, and to the side were white paper streamers used as purification wands.

Stuck to the wall was a map of the world, and like the globe I had seen on my first visit, the map was full of tiny pins with red heads. The teacher took out a pointer, placed it on the map and began talking to the group kneeling on the wooden floor in front of him.

"The pins are where gods have been placed. Now he is telling about your placing of the god in Florida," whispered Kazz, who sat next to me. "Very interesting. He says that where you put the god was exactly in the middle between North and South America. It is also where the god world meets the human world. He says the tornado occurred because of this meeting of heaven and earth. Go! He is calling for you."

Kazz gently pushed me forward. All I recognized was my name when the teacher talked, but when he finished the

group clapped and then bowed. I felt as though I were in
school and receiving a reward for something I had said or
done—only I wasn't quite sure what it was I was being re-
warded for. I faced the group, returned their claps and bows,
and returned to the back of the room. I realized in a rush that
all these followers knew about the project.

The teacher went to the shrine, and everyone turned toward him. The fluorescent lights were turned off, and he lit
candles. In the eerie glow, I looked at Kazz and barely recognized him. He had closed his eyes and pulled a huge sword
from a sheath. Where did the sword come from? He raised it
high over his head and waved it. It was a real sword, razor
sharp, the kind that cut and hurt and killed. It wasn't broken.
It wasn't metaphorical. Kazz looked like a furious samurai
fighting a bloody battle. I looked around and saw other
warriors waving their just-as-real swords in the flickering light.
They chanted words that I could not understand.

"What the hell?" I muttered to myself. "This is nuts."

The smiles were gone, replaced by pained, agonized
looks. The tempo and volume of the chanting increased. I
glanced nervously at the distorted faces that surrounded me.
I smelled sweat. I checked my tape recorder to insure that it
was working and snapped pictures of the oblivious participants. At the back of the room, the women waved smaller
daggers with the same intense look on their faces. I later
learned that what looked like daggers were holy objects in
daggerlike form.

The teacher sat near the altar, his eyes closed and his chin slightly turned up. He was mumbling and seemed far away from the events in the room. Suddenly someone in the back blew a whistle, and everyone lowered their swords. A quiet chanting ensued. The sound reminded me of a bubbling stream, and I was momentarily calmed. But then, several minutes later, the whistle blew again. The swords were raised once again in the air, accompanied by more frantic yelling and waving.

This was repeated four times and lasted about 25 minutes in all. Afterward, following a brief break in which people sat exhausted on the floor, names were called by a participant in the front of the room. One by one, people went forward and placed leafy branches as offerings at the door of the wooden shrine. I heard my name called, and when I went to the front of the room, I did everything wrong. I was so bewildered by everyone's transformation into warriors that I knelt in the wrong place, offered the branch backward, and placed it in the wrong pile. I managed to get a bow and a clap in before I returned to the back of the room and turned toward the teacher.

"Tonight I went to Russia," said the teacher, his voice once again commanding all of our attention. "I saw a dark cloud over the Kremlin. Your chanting broke the cloud, and God's breath came through. It was a very difficult fight, and we didn't get through completely. I saw the Kremlin in ruins and a temple being built to replace it."

How unlikely, I thought. The Soviet Empire has existed for more than 65 years, through my lifetime and my father's lifetime. It would take a nuclear war to destroy it, and I didn't think the teacher meant he had initiated such a disaster. The Kremlin replaced by a temple? The Soviet Union officially disavowed all religious beliefs. It would take a major philosophical shift for that to happen.

After the teacher's description the participants disrobed, dressed, and, in another room, struck up easy, relaxed conversation.

"What was that all about?" I asked Kazz when he finally joined me.

"We call it a fighting ceremony," he replied. "We meet once a month."

"Just these people? No one else from the group I met last time?"

"A few more. But only the most powerful. The teacher always travels different places. This month it was the Soviet Union, last month it was China. He has traveled to the places where the gods were placed, taking with him the collective energy of the group. We are his soldiers, battling the bad spirits that engulf the earth."

"Where do *you* go?" I asked. "Your face…"

"It's like a dream. I have little memory," Kazz said. "I don't know."

Kazz was anxious to leave for home. Once in the car he was unusually talkative. He told me he and his wife Tazuko had reconciled their problems and were living together again. His three daughters were now very happy. Everyone was sorry that Donna wasn't along and that I could only stay for a couple days. He was excited for me that the teacher had singled me out for my placing in Florida, and that I should consider it an honor. And, finally, he said, handing me an envelope, "The teacher gave me this to give to you."

As I reached for the envelope, my mind was filled with the image of the powerful warriors waving real swords, battling an invisible enemy. I opened it and found several ten-thousand-yen notes—about five hundred dollars.

"What's this for?" I asked.

"For your help. Travel is expensive, no?"

I quickly slipped the money back into the envelope and pushed it into Kazz's lap. I felt confused. I knew the Japanese are fond of giving presents, but this was excessive, although I could certainly use it. I felt I didn't deserve it.

"Please find a way to give this back to the teacher without insulting him. It's just not the way I do things."

chapter 12

A miniature replica of the original Sword
of Heaven.

Don't you understand what I'm tryin' to say,
An' can't you feel the fears I'm feelin' today?
If the button is pushed, there's no runnin' away,
There'll be no one to save, with the world in a grave.
Take a look around you, boy, it's bound to scare you, boy.
An' you tell me, over and over and over again, my friend,
Ah, you don't believe we're on the eve of destruction.

—"The Eve of Destruction" sung by Barry McGuire, 1965's number one song (P. F. Sloan)

Juan Li, with his usual good timing, was waiting for me in
San Francisco. He was visiting from Oaxaca, Mexico, where
he now lived. Donna had told him my schedule, and he had
postponed his return trip so we could get together. We met

a day after I returned, at Donna's spacious loft in the old Sears and Roebuck building.

I sank exhausted into the couch. Donna, after talking with us briefly, excused herself to another part of the loft that had once contained the former department store's garden and tool department. She had paintings to complete, and she'd already heard an account of my travels. She also knew I needed time alone with Juan Li, who, unlike Kazz, always seemed able to answer my questions.

After she left, I immediately told Juan about the death threats, the tornado in Florida, the fear I experienced in the Philippines, and the frightening sword-waving scene I had just witnessed in Japan. I told him how I had refused the money the teacher offered me, but readily accepted the four gods Kazz had asked me to take back to San Francisco.

Juan Li smiled. "They never offered me money."

"Made me feel like a mercenary or something," I responded.

"The group has money, you know. I'm sure they help Kazz."

"Not that I couldn't use it," I said. "But with my doubts about everything it just wouldn't be right."

"But you accepted four more gods?" he asked.

"Don't ask me to explain. I also accepted this."

I handed Juan a small package. It contained a pair of miniature swords, not much bigger than kitchen knives. They were exact replicas of the original Sword of Heaven.

Kazz had commissioned a famous sword maker to make three: one for him, one for Juan, and one for me. Juan handled the package carefully, clearly impressed with the gift.

"How is my old friend Kazz?" he asked. "I haven't heard from him in months."

"He seems fine," I answered. "Drives me crazy with his inscrutable act. But I'm almost used to it."

Juan looked thoughtful. "When I first met Kazz he was very impatient. He was also full of pride and ego. I always felt that the teacher gave Kazz the task of placing the gods to help mold his personality."

"He has definitely mellowed since I first met him," I said.

"Sounds like the project has taken some of the edge off him," Juan continued after a few moments. "Polished him. Given him a sense of purpose and a larger view of the world."

"What about you?" I asked Juan. "What are you getting out of this project?"

He hesitated.

In the silence I realized that if Juan had any emotional confusion or doubts about the Shinto project, he never showed them. His interest seemed more theological or intellectual.

His belated response confirmed my impression: "I'm very interested in Shinto. It's the last great Eastern religion to be closely examined by the West. I also like that Shinto demands respect for nature...."

"Nothing personal then, eh?" I asked.

"Not like you." As he grinned, I saw in him a confident, older brother, getting pleasure from watching me and Kazz and others grow through our struggles.

"Before I forget," Juan added quickly, "I need one of the gods. A friend—an American Indian—wants to take one to New Mexico, to the Trinity site where they tested the first A-bomb. I promised him one."

"Sure. It's yours. They're all yours if you want."

Juan declined, saying he didn't have room in his luggage and that he would write if he planned on traveling somewhere where one was needed. I agreed to send the god to his friend.

Just then I felt the floor beneath my feet vibrate. Juan looked concerned.

"Don't worry, it's not an earthquake," I said laughing. "This building sits on top of a BART tunnel. A train just passed underneath."

When I first started seeing Donna, there were other noises as well. Her loft was on the corner of two of the busiest streets in the city, Army and Mission. The sounds from cars honking, tires squealing, boom boxes blasting, and late-night reverie filled the bedroom until I bought $\frac{1}{2}$-inch Plexiglas sheets and covered the windows. Even then, I couldn't really get a good night's sleep unless we stayed at my house, which was nearby but close to a quiet park. Donna had a higher tolerance for chaotic surroundings, and her indifference to noise was becoming an issue for me.

The vibration stopped and I asked Juan, "So what do you think of the tornado after the placing in Florida? Coincidence? Why the deaths, the violence?"

"You've tried acupuncture?" he responded.

"After the car accident, to relieve the swelling in my wrist. It worked great."

"The Chinese believe that there are channels of energy crisscrossing the earth, much like in the human body. They call them dragon veins. Well, think of the sword as an acupuncture needle, and you hit one powerful vein. Recovery isn't always pretty."

"And the Philippines?"

"The project does seem to have a mind of its own, doesn't it?" Juan said. "Who knows what that boy was thinking? Maybe he thought you were planting a listening device for the military island. Or maybe he is deathly afraid of the Japanese. Or..." his voice trailed off. "The Filipinos are a superstitious lot. Maybe he felt what you were doing and it scared him. Don't worry about it."

"Don't worry about it!" I cried. "I could get hurt."

Juan looked puzzled at my strong reaction. "Okay," he said, "What do you think?"

"I have no idea. But I'm going crazy thinking about it. I even considered bad spirits."

"Bad spirits? Oh, I remember, Kazz's warning. But I thought you didn't believe in them."

"I didn't use to," I said.

Juan looked amused.

Exasperated, I added, "But strange things keep happening."

I recounted to Juan my experience in the bomb shelter just before I tried to place a god at the Lab and my resulting ambivalence, and the storm on Mount Shasta.

"And now you suspect bad spirits?"

I shrugged.

"That's what the teacher said," I said finally. "But I don't know what I believe. When you first told me about the project, you told me the Sword of Heaven was broken. I liked the idea—swords into plowshares, that sort of thing. But I didn't get it right, did I? The opposite was true. Each piece, each god, represents another complete sword, doesn't it?"

"I suppose so," Juan said.

"And now there are many more swords engaged in a battle, right? That's not very peaceful."

"No one is getting hurt, though," Juan answered. "Unless you consider what happened in Florida."

"I always thought of Eastern religions as monks in quiet meditation, impervious to what was happening around them. Contained in their own world."

"Not Shinto," replied Juan. "You've certainly heard that Japan is full of artists and warriors, haven't you?"

"Samurai stuff. Yeah. It's a cliché by now."

"But there's a lot of truth in it. They've really developed the warrior mentality. It's been translated into 'aggressive marketing' in the modern world. Never resting. Always marching forward. Action."

"Fighting for peace never made sense to me," I replied.

"But it's all done ritualistically!" laughed Juan. "It's all about mental discipline. It's an art to train the mind to respond in an active, positive way to events. The warrior energy gets things done. Think of Joan of Arc, think of Jesus in the Temple with the money changers. It's an energy that you access. It doesn't control you. You control it. There is nothing wrong with warrior energy when it's used consciously. It's only when it's not that all sorts of evil things result."

"Like during World War II. The atrocities in China, in Manchuria—the Japanese have a tendency to get out of control, don't they?"

"Could be, yeah."

I looked out the window for a minute. It was true: this aspect of the Japanese had bothered me from the beginning. They seemed to be perpetually in motion, like an engine stuck on full steam ahead. When did they stop to reflect?

Then I said to Juan Li: "Maybe that's why the teacher was so impressed with Jesus when he met him."

Juan looked confused, and I told him about the teacher meeting Christ and hearing about the "great love."

"He was so impressed," I repeated.

"Strange that it would seem so radical to him. Shinto isn't only about swords and action, you know."

"I know, the teacher told me about the mirror and the jewel. The mirror symbolizes self-knowledge; the jewel, compassion. But I'm telling you, the idea of universal love spoke powerfully to him."

Juan laughed. "I just had a thought. Japan needs to learn about this kind of love, and you need to learn about the warrior."

I slumped into the couch, my mind elsewhere. "Growing up in suburbia, with a scientist father, hardly prepared me for all of this. It's such a stretch."

"If you stretch too fast, you'll hurt yourself. Sounds like you need some time out."

I agreed, at the same time motioning in Donna's direction. "Donna and I have friends in New York who want to sublet us their studio during the winter. She's always wanted to try New York. It would be good to get away."

"New York!" Juan's eyes gleamed. "I've lived there. Yes, go there. Maybe it will give you the perspective you need."

Although I didn't feel completely decided, I grabbed onto Juan Li's encouragement in much the same way I soaked up the teacher's advice on my first visit to Japan. I craved direction, and perhaps the move could give me that.

chapter 13

A view from our East Village loft.

During the winter of 1986 the space shuttle Challenger
*exploded, showering the Atlantic with pieces of metal and flesh
and the optimism and dreams of a generation. On the other side of
the world, in another explosion, Chernobyl began to rain
radioactivity over central and northern Europe.*

*In the Philippines, at the end of February, nine months after I
placed a god there, dictator Ferdinand Marcos was ousted in a
peaceful democratic election, which brought the populist leader
Corazon Aquino to power. For the first time, I saw a connection
between the Sword of Heaven and a peaceful world event.*

I had arrived in Manhattan on the last day of 1985. Donna had flown out a few weeks earlier while I had crossed the country alone in a Mercury Marquis drive-away filled with my camera equipment, computer, and all the other things I needed to continue my freelance business in New York. On Juan Li's suggestion I had brought along one of the three remaining Shinto gods in my possession. While it was possible but unlikely that I would have the opportunity to personally place the god, I figured that Juan or someone else might need it. I drove across Arizona, New Mexico, Texas, and the Southeast to avoid the frozen north, and five days after I left my home in San Francisco, I crossed the Holland Tunnel onto the island.

Following Donna's directions, I drove to 390 East Sixth Street. It was immediately apparent to me that this was not a great neighborhood. Police were on every corner, slapping themselves vigorously to keep away the cold. Yellow streetlights illuminated cheap tenement housing in varying degrees of decay. Incongruously I also saw newly built condos with such pretentious statements engraved in the facades as "Built in 1984." Everywhere I looked there were condemned houses and vacant lots.

After I parked the travel-soiled car, one of the policemen strolled over, noticed the California plates and then peered into the packed car. He said that I shouldn't stay long, that if I hadn't noticed this wasn't a safe area. I pointed across the street to a four-story building and said, "That's my new home."

He looked at the low, rusty iron fence, at the glassless windows protected by iron grates, at the piles of garbage and the loose brick surrounding the building. Then he looked back at me and shook his head.

At that moment Donna poked her head through the steel-reinforced double door, waved, and yelled nervously that we should get my things inside quickly. The amused policeman watched as we toted all my valuable equipment across the street and into the building.

"We're on the fourth floor," Donna said. "No elevator."

I looked back to the car and watched the policeman walk back to his corner. A head appeared at an apartment window across the street, then quickly disappeared. Someone shouted in Spanish.

Inside, a single bulb barely lit the four flights of stairs. Linoleum peeled from the floor, and the smell of heating fuel was everywhere.

"The first floor is a social service agency for battered women and family counseling," Donna said as we dragged my stuff up the wide stairs. "The women who run the program are gone for the holidays."

On the dimly lit landing of the second floor, a huge man appeared. I took a deep breath. Donna greeted him by name and introduced me as her friend. "Bo" gripped my hand with a bear-sized palm and said, "Hi, blondie," with a grin. Glancing past him through the open door, I saw a pool table and a Ping-Pong table. Bo, it turned out, ran the New Life after-school program for neighborhood children. On a normal day, the place would be packed. Bo locked the door and carried his heavy frame down the stairs, wishing us a Happy New Year as he went.

"Don't talk with anyone on the third floor," Donna whispered as we continued up. The third floor was a half-way house run by the Lower East Side Church, which also rented a room downstairs near the social services offices to use for Sunday worship. As we walked quietly past the third floor, I caught the scent of marijuana. Then someone cried out in a loud, piercing voice, "Ziggy! Ziggy!" A voice screeched back in answer, a voice that only could have come from living too long in places where no one listened. I cringed. What a hungry voice!

"Come on," Donna said, "let's get out of here. These guys give me the creeps."

Our loft was nearly as big as a basketball court, with windows that looked out to four breathtaking views of Manhattan. From one window I could see the Empire State Building, its top lit with green lights to celebrate the season. Visible out the back was the Hudson river and the Williamsburg Bridge. Donna had divided the space. The walls on her side were bare so that she could hang her paintings. On my side was a long table which I could use as a desk and to organize my photographic prints and slides. I set up my computer and then rested a picture of Mount Shasta against it. Donna's friends had left behind all the amenities we needed to make the loft quite livable including cooking utensils, a stereo, two televisions, and several phones.

After the holidays there weren't as many police prowling the streets, but behind the steel door, at the top of four flights of stairs, we felt relatively safe. At first it seemed easy to forget the outside world. We got along with the building's other occupants, except for those on the third floor, whom we tried to ignore. Donna painted and spent countless hours visiting art galleries and museums. Her work, I noticed, was turning from harsh black-and-white images to paintings with softer, more sensual shapes and even color. She was able, it seemed, to create some peace in the middle of the crazy city. I spent my time on the phone arranging meetings with art directors and magazine editors, trying to hustle work.

Outside our loft, however, was a war zone. Broken glass sprinkled the street, and there were random signs of violence everywhere. Mutilating phones was a particularly popular activity, and I saw lots of bashed receivers with wires dangling from the black plastic handles. One day I walked past at least fifteen police cars converged on a group of five or six teenagers, and that night the evening news reported it as the largest crack bust in U.S. history.

A month after I arrived, the armored front door downstairs was torn off its hinges. The people on the third floor blamed the people on the second floor, who in turn blamed the people on the third. Whoever did it must have been desperate to get in because the door was solid steel. The damage amounted to $2,000, and the absentee landlord was in no hurry to repair it.

Without the front door, the outside world rushed in. The third floor went from a halfway house to a flop house. The hungry screams of Ziggy grew as he tried to control his new friends. To get to the fourth floor, I regularly stepped over unconscious drunks and around ranting crack addicts.

Even the house groaned under the new load. Inside our loft, particularly on a cold day, the radiator pipes began to rattle like an engine ready to die. As if this weren't enough, demolition crews moved into the neighborhood. During breaks in the winter storms, huge cranes with steel bashing balls pounded condemned houses into rubble, making room for new buildings. When they were finished, the pile drivers arrived. Our building shook with the tremors as walls of brick crashed to the frozen ground and pile drivers pounded away. It was impossible to make phone calls during business hours, and finding work proved nearly impossible.

"Donna, this is the worst," I said one day in despair.

"We can't leave. What about Steve and Sheila's stuff?"

"The city is falling apart. I can't stand it."

"It's not the city; it's here, this house, this neighborhood."

"It feels like the entire city."

"I don't know what to do. Maybe you should try not to take it so personally."

"Right," I answered sarcastically. I was hating New York. Nothing could have been further from my protective

childhood bomb shelter than our fourth story loft, exposed
to all the violence and noise of the city. I felt tremendously
vulnerable and at my wit's end. I felt as though I were on a
ship that had just sprung a huge leak and I was drowning
along with everyone else.

Then I received a letter from Juan's Native American
friend, Turtle Heart. He had successfully placed a god at the
Trinity test site, in the New Mexican desert where the first
atomic bomb was exploded on July 16, 1945. His letter,
which was also addressed to Kazz, was twelve typewritten
pages long. I read about his difficult but ultimately successful
placing and felt a kinship with him. He said it was the most
difficult episode of his life.

Turtle Heart decided to follow a Native American
practice and first circled the area around the nuclear test site
before ritually placing the god. The circle turned out to be
350 miles in circumference, which he drove by car. After a
few days of preparation he parked the car, packed the kami
and sacred pipes and a deer antler, and walked into the desert
toward the Trinity site. He walked nine hours. It grew dark
and very cold. He napped and then donned his ceremonial
dress. After a brief ceremony, he planted the god in the area

he determined was the site of the first nuclear blast. On his return, in the middle of the night, he was stopped by White Sands Missile Range security police. He told them he was a lost hiker. He was detained for four hours and after a security check he was driven back to his car. "As I crossed the Rio Grande River," he wrote, "twenty miles west of where I started, I had a tremendous emotional release, and I wept and sobbed and knew I was both afraid and amazed at this life and this place... I believe I left a physical piece of my own flesh on this land... I went north to Taos Pueblo and rested with the Elders for two days."

I couldn't understand why our government has made it so hard for someone like Turtle Heart to make a pilgrimage to the spot where the atomic age began. I knew that the site was only open to the public twice a year, in April and October, and not on the actual July 16th date when the first bomb was successfully exploded. I knew that even when it is open to the public, no banners, no speeches, no outpouring of expression are allowed. Ground Zero should be a public monument, just like the Washington monument in Washington, D.C. It should be a place where anyone at anytime could pay homage to the powerful nuclear forces that changed the world.

Turtle Heart's letter made me keenly aware of my inaction in New York and my sense of helplessness. After my successful placing in Florida, I had hoped my life would flow more smoothly, or that I would at least feel it had a clearer direction. Instead, I was once again unfocused, without any sense of momentum from the project, my relationship with Donna, or my work.

One day, at the end of February, I was in Midtown hurrying to a meeting with the art director of Forbes, my portfolio under my arm. I waited for the light to turn.

The night before, Ziggy and his gang had been particularly wild. Someone had pounded furiously on the door of our flat, prompting me to barricade the door with a chair. I lay awake all night, worrying that someone would nonetheless manage to push the door open. Now, staring at the red light, I felt totally drained and vulnerable.

I caught a nauseating odor of urine from the man standing next to me. I turned to look at him. His clothes were tattered and his crotch was wet. I looked at him a moment too long and his eyes caught mine.

What eyes! They seemed to be black, bottomless pits, absorbing me into their emptiness. They fixed on me intently, and I felt caught in their glare. It took all my strength to tear my eyes away from his and run into the middle of Fifth Avenue, nearly into the path of an oncoming taxi.

As I stumbled through the cacophony of honking horns

and projectiles of steel and glass, I could hear the madman behind me screaming.

"You! Hey, you! You bastard! Come back!"

"You look terrible," Donna said when I got home. "What happened? How did your meeting go?"

I told her about my encounter with the madman, which inexplicably was haunting me. I didn't even mention the business meeting, which hadn't gone well anyway.

"Why did you look at him? You know better."

"I was so tired."

"You look awful. I'm really worried about you."

"I'm okay. Anyway, the poor guy was harmless."

Donna looked at me carefully.

"Are you sure you're okay?"

"I'm tired, that's all."

What could I say? Clearly Donna loved New York. She had jumped into the city with both feet, and the city had responded, inspiring her work and giving it a meaningful context. Donna complained about the weather and the day-to-day grind of living in Manhattan just like everyone else, but at the same time she blossomed. While I wished I were someplace else.

That night my bomb shelter nightmare returned. I was

facing the escape hatch of the bomb shelter. I was filled with
fear. But this time I actually moved close enough to the hatch
door to touch it. I tried to open it, but then the evil started
screaming; this time, the voice was the voice of the madman
on the street. I froze, no longer able to move. I woke covered
in sweat and breathing heavily. I pushed Donna, who was
gently touching me, away.

One day in March all the noise stopped. I looked out the
window and saw huge flakes of snow swirling around the
blackened buildings, winter's final storm. Within a few hours
the snow transformed the streets. The construction crews
stayed home. The boiler, as it often did on cold days, ran out
of fuel, and the radiator stopped its insufferable clanging. The
door had been fixed and the third floor was quiet. Donna had
an appointment with an art dealer, and I was alone in a still,
cold room. Steam vapors from my breath hung in the air.

It was noon, and I was quietly editing a batch of photographs I had taken the week before. Finishing, I washed
my hands and put Grieg's "Per Gynt Suite" on the turn-
table, sitting on a makeshift couch of cushions piled on the
floor and against the wall. I sighed and turned my attention
to the sad violin in the piece entitled "In the Hall of the
Mountain King."

As the music filled the stillness, I was overcome by an eerie feeling. My body became all breath: it didn't have any substance, just a throat and lungs. At first I liked the feeling. I was so light! But then I got nervous. Would the feeling end? Would my breath and my body remain forever disconnected? Would I go insane?

I stretched out on the couch. I no longer heard the music.

I concentrated on taking a deep, slow breath.

And then another.

Now I could feel the rest of my body. As each breath rolled into my lungs I was aware of my feet, my ankles, my knees, even my hips. Then the breath moved to my chest, where I felt my heart pounding.

"Stay deep," I said to myself. "Don't come up."

Out of the breath came the lake in Norway, my father at my side. My hand was outstretched, with the heavy god and its white cloth with strange symbols in such contrast to the calm lake and evergreens. I felt very strong and safe.

Then the madman's face replaced the idyllic scene. For a second I stopped breathing, frozen by the terror he instilled in me. I saw in him a part of me, the part of me that didn't know what it was doing or where it was going. And I knew that if I didn't figure things out soon, I might go completely mad, just like the man on the street.

Then I saw the teacher's face, and Kazz and the others. I saw their determination and the pain of the fighting ceremony as if they too were reaching to that lake and then here to our leaking ship on the Lower East Side. The wild sword-waving ceremony I witnessed in Japan was no longer threatening. Instead I felt its purpose and direction, and I felt connected to the warriors.

I suddenly understood the Shinto project differently. It was an elaborate ritual in which, if I chose, I could explore the depths of my unconscious without fear of annihilation. It was a watertight container in which both my rational and intuitive minds could relax and perhaps even come to an understanding. It was like one of Donna's frames, which gave her work a defined beginning and end in space. The project was a vessel that would carry me safely to my destination, a destination that I hoped I would soon comprehend.

I decided that it wasn't necessary for me to fully understand the spirit world of Shinto, or to reconcile its contradictions with my ingrained Western beliefs. I could still have my doubts and participate in the project.

With these thoughts I found in myself a new momentum. The project must be finished—if not for Kazz or the teacher or the world, then for me. It had to become my top priority, above everything. When it came to the Sword of Heaven, from now on I would put both my feet forward.

By the end of the symphony, the snow had stopped, and I could hear Ziggy's obnoxious voice below. The boiler was chattering again. I heard Donna on the stairs.

I went to the bookshelf and pulled out an atlas, looking for the right spot to place the next god.

PART THREE

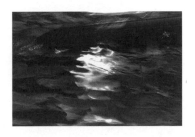

Things
that have affinity
in their inmost natures
seek one another.

chapter 14

Lake Lögurinn in southeast Iceland,
where I placed the god.

*On April 5, 1986, at a popular disco in West Berlin, a bomb
exploded and killed two American servicemen and a young
Turkish woman and wounded 229 others. A few weeks later, on
April 14th, the United States launched a carefully calculated air
attack against targets in Libya claiming Libya's involvement in the
Berlin bombings. To many observers both the disco bombing and
the U.S. air attacks were bold and provocative and only fueled the
fear that the fate of the world hung in a precarious balance.*

When I called Donna from my hotel in Reykjavík, I was
looking at snowcapped mountains, imagining her view of
garbage and waste. When I told her that the river that flowed
through the middle of the capital was full of salmon and was

so pure you could drink from it, I felt guilty. She had wanted to come. But if both of us had left, our friends' loft would have been picked clean.

After the five-hour flight, I slept for a day, more from the exhaustion of the last five months than from jet lag. I chose Iceland to place the next god simply because it was the first place that caught my eye when I opened the atlas, but as I woke to an Arctic silence, I could already feel strength flowing back into my limbs and spirit.

Although I had been to Iceland before, I had never ventured from Reykjavík, the capital. This time, on the suggestion of a friendly Icelandic travel agent, I planned to fly north across the barren center to Akureyri in the far north and then hop southeast along the coast, mostly taking planes like the locals because of the rugged land. My seven-day itinerary would give me a good overview of the island, and take me to several possible sites for placing the Shinto god.

Lake Myvatn, in the north, famous for its bird life and fishing, was my first stop. A spring blizzard began just after I left Akureyri in my rental car, and none of the fishermen I asked would even consider taking me out on the still partly frozen lake.

From my hotel window, I caught occasional glimpses through the snow of a huge volcanic caldera, near the lake. Most of Iceland is volcanically active with eruptions occurring on average every five years. A volcano seemed like an appropriate location for a god, especially after my unsuccessful attempt on Mount Shasta. I waited for the clouds to lift.

When the blizzard finally subsided I drove to the volcano's base. I packed the god in my day pack and walked up the steep wall to the rim, past gaping fissures that exuded sulfur gas. The wind was so strong and cold that I walked with my mittens up over my face. Now and then, an orange sun poked through the overcast sky, and I could see deep into the rocky bottom of the caldera. Steam hissed from the interior. I dropped down into the caldera to escape the wind and sat on a heated rock. I heard a low rumbling: I thought at first it was a jet but then realized it was the wind blowing over the edge, like the sound a kid makes blowing on a soda bottle.

The thought of planes stirred memories of the first time I flew to Iceland, when I was nine, on my way to Norway with my younger brother Erik. Our prop plane developed engine trouble and was forced to land in Reykjavík. We were on the ground for 24 hours before continuing on to Oslo. As two young boys traveling alone, we were doted on by everyone.

I still cherish memories of that Norwegian summer. We spent every day fishing, hiking, and playing in the countryside. We made a simple raft from logs and rope after we saw Thor Heyerdahl's *Kon Tiki* in a museum in Oslo. The Norwegian explorers were my heroes: Heyerdahl, who sailed the *Kon Tiki* across the Pacific from Peru; Roald Amundsen,

who discovered the South Pole; Fridtjof Nansen, who tried
to reach the North Pole on skis; and, of course, Leif Eriksson,
discoverer of both Iceland and North America. I had wanted
more than anything an adventure of my own—on, of course,
a boat. At the end of the idyllic summer we flew home to
Livermore to my father building the bomb shelter, the
Cuban missile crisis, and the start of my recurring nightmare.

Now, sitting in Iceland on the edge of a volcano, it
occurred to me that I was on an adventure not so different
from my childhood fantasy. I'd traveled to exotic locales and
met strange and magical people. There was even a boat, albeit
only in a vision. My destination didn't involve new worlds or
scientific discovery, but my goal still felt noble: I wanted to
make some contribution to world peace.

As I grabbed the Shinto god from my pack, I realized that
there was something else. I wanted to be happy like I was that
summer so long ago in Norway. I didn't want to live in a
world of fear.

Nothing held me back from placing the god on the volcano. I just felt it wasn't the right place or the right time. I
was only halfway through my itinerary and knew there
would be other opportunities.

I continued by plane southeast to Egilsstadir, a small
town located on the oldest geological part of Iceland. Unlike most of the rest of the island, the area around Egilsstadir
is geologically stable. Although the town has only a few hundred inhabitants, its geographic location makes it a crossroads

of sorts. There is an airport with regular flights to Greenland and the Faroe Islands, several gas stations and hotels to service the heavy tourist traffic during the summer months, and just a few miles east in Seydisfjördur, a deepwater harbor where ferries leave for Norway, the ancestral home of all the island's inhabitants, as well as Britain.

All the hotels in town were full, but I found a room nearby on the shores of Lake Lögurinn in a private farmhouse. That night, sitting at a massive wooden table, my host told me in perfect English that the area had been considered a major crossroads even before the arrival of airplanes and cars. The legendary Norse gods Thor and Odin were said to meet here regularly, finding it a convenient spot.

"Oh, we have lots of legends," she said when she saw my interest. "In fact," she said proudly, "did you know we have our own Loch Ness monster? Every time there is a sighting, something awful happens in the world. The last time was just before World War II. But if you want to know more about legends you must talk with Jøn Loftsson, the ranger in charge of the forest. He lives in the middle of the forest with his Norwegian wife and two children."

"Forest?" I asked, puzzled. Except for private gardens, so far I had only seen bare, moonlike landscapes.

"The largest in Iceland," she said. At that moment, the other overnight guests, a Norwegian woman and her traveling companion, walked in. The landlady turned her attention to them, and as I made my way upstairs to my room I heard her explaining that yes, the picture on the wall was Prince Charles. He had once stopped for lunch here.

The next afternoon, under cloudy skies, I drove along the lake and found Loftsson's house. The low structure was surrounded by trees I learned were Siberian larch. The family was just settling down for a hearty lamb stew and invited me to join them. We never got around to talk about Icelandic legends: instead, Loftsson's ten-year-old son wanted to hear everything I knew about Native American Indians. Then Loftsson told me about historical Iceland and his dream for the future.

"Today Iceland is only 1 percent forest," he said in English, "but a thousand years ago, when the Vikings arrived, it was 25 percent forest and a virtual paradise. There were abundant fish and forest animals. No one went hungry. The winters were long and dark, but the Gulf Stream kept the average temperature warmer than New York or Vienna.

"The Vikings built huge mansions and heated them with entire tree trunks. They also brought sheep with them. The Vikings knocked down the trees, and the sheep did their best to keep any saplings from replacing the depleted forest.

"It took only 200 years for the paradise to be spoiled. Without fuel, Icelanders could only scratch out a meager living. They were isolated from the Dark Ages, the Renaissance, and the Industrial Revolution. There was little reason for Europeans to visit Iceland, and the culture became fixed in time."

After lunch we took a stroll and Loftsson showed me the tiny saplings growing nearby. There were only 800 hectares, but one day, he believed strongly, the entire valley would be forested again.

We came to a fence. The larch and birch abruptly stopped, and on the other side was a denuded stretch of land filled with low scrub; it looked like the face of a man who shaves with a dull blade. "Sheep," Loftsson mumbled disdainfully, as he handed me a tiny pinecone, the size of my thumbnail.

Holding the tiny cone in my hand, I realized that like me, Loftsson was a man on a mission. But there was something fundamentally different between me and him. He had a beautiful family and a dream that was quantifiable. While I was trying to plant metaphorical seeds of peace, he was planting real seeds, and getting tangible results. I envied him and felt an intense pang of loneliness.

That night at dinner at a nearby restaurant I drank too much red wine. Afterward, at my landlady's farmhouse, I grabbed the Shinto god and took it to the edge of the lake. It was late in the evening, and cold. There was no one outside, although I saw a figure in a farmhouse window far away. A solitary bird flew overhead. The wine had intensified my loneliness. Despite the hour, it was still light and far across the lake a streak of snow reached down from a single cloud like a tentacle to lightly brush across the surface of the lake. For a moment I saw the cloud as the head of a giant monster and the waving shape underneath as its ominous body. I remembered my host's story, and I briefly wondered if this was a sign that something awful was going to happen in the world.

I pulled back my arm to toss the Shinto god into the lake. From the back of my throat two words formed: Thor! Odin! As my arm snapped forward, the words sprang from my lips and flew with the god as it sailed through the air. Both the god and my words traveled much farther than I expected.

Two more birds flew overhead and playfully darted back and forth across the lake. Uninhibited from the wine, I waved my hands in the air, imagining I was one of them.

"Well, look who has arrived," I cried. "There's Juan, the older brother! And Kazz, the inscrutable!"

I started waving my hands again. "Welcome to the meeting place of the gods! Welcome!"

We danced together, the three of us. We were gods! We danced to a score conceived and conducted by a wise old man who claimed to be an instrument of God himself.

We danced for the world. We danced for ourselves. We pounded our feet on the ground until the earth shook. We cried to the heavens, to our fellow gods. We laughed. Nothing was serious, except our pleasure. For a few glorious moments, I forgot that Kazz was the mysterious East, I the rational West, and Juan, well, Juan with his Cuban and Chinese blood was the cool middle man. I forgot all our differences and danced madly with them as brothers.

"Old man," I thought as I finally stopped and focused blurry-eyed across the lake. "You are as confusing as hell, but your music is beautiful, and it is a wonderful night in Iceland!"

On the way back to my room, I patted the landlady's sheep dog's head as he bounded up to greet me. I crawled into bed and fell asleep immediately. I woke just past midnight—my throat dry, my head aching, and my right arm sore from throwing the heavy stone. What had gotten into me? Dancing drunk on the shore like that. Thinking I was a god? The resolve to finish the project I had felt in New York dimmed like the evening sky, and I wondered what the hell I was doing spending so much time and money to toss a stone into a lake, so far from home.

"Get a real job," I scolded myself. "Get a life. Settle in the country, have a family, and plant trees."

My negativity passed, and I heard the cries of the three birds again as I fell asleep.

chapter 15

My German friend Wolfgang
at the Berlin Wall.

"It'll be a cold winter."

—President Kennedy in 1961 when Soviet Premier Khrushchev threatened
nuclear war over Berlin

Soon after I returned from Iceland, Donna and I got into a
serious argument. Our sublet was nearly up. I was disgusted
with the violence and intensity of the building and the
neighborhood, and I told her that I wanted to go back to
San Francisco, where I could make some money and get
some rest. She wanted to stay in New York and pursue her
career. We came to an uneasy compromise. She'd find another place, in a safer neighborhood, and I would return to
San Francisco, fatten my bank account, and then come back

to New York. In the meantime we'd maintain a bicoastal relationship.

After New York, San Francisco seemed like a village. Strangers were friendly. Taxi drivers were polite. "It's almost too nice," I said to Donna on the phone after a week. "I'm getting nervous. The other day, when I was swimming at the pool, this guy got in my way and I laid into him. Told him what I thought. He just crumbled and looked at me like I was crazy."

"Marshmallows," said Donna.

"Yeah, but you know, it's so nice to be able to sleep at night without someone trying to break in."

The summer passed. Donna flew out to the West Coast to see me. I flew to New York to see her. In the meantime, I tried to hustle assignments that would take me to places that lacked a Shinto god.

In the fall, Diversion magazine assigned me to write an article on Helsinki. Gods had already been placed in Finland, according to Kazz, but none in the Baltic Sea. Also, he said in answer to my query, none had been placed in Berlin.

In the late afternoon of October 21, 1986, my old friend Wolfgang met me at the Hamburg train station. Finnair had flown me as their guest from Seattle to Helsinki and then on to Copenhagen. There I boarded a train bound for West Germany. Wolfgang had parked illegally, and we hurried to his car, a 1967 Mercedes station wagon. He pushed boxes full of his movie equipment and film aside and tossed my luggage, including two gods, into the backseat. The rain was relentless and the rush-hour traffic overwhelming. Nonetheless, we decided to leave immediately for Berlin and eat later.

"How's Donna?" he asked after successfully navigating us out of the congested city. He'd met her a couple times, once in San Francisco and once in New York.

"She's fine. She loves New York, which is a problem." Wolfgang nodded.

"It's a great city," I quickly added, "but difficult."

"I know. But you are in San Francisco now, right?"

"I've been flying back and forth."

"Will you move back to New York?"

"That's the plan," I said with false enthusiasm, "as soon as I can." In fact, the very thought of living in New York again depressed me. But if I didn't return, what would happen to Donna and me? And what about the Shinto project? It was getting harder and harder to juggle the project, the relationship, and the rest of my life.

"Why are you here, in Europe?" Wolfgang asked after a pause, unaware of my internal conflict. "Why Berlin?"

I explained that I was on assignment but that I was interested in Berlin because of the Shinto peace project. Like all my close friends, he already knew about my involvement. I had been at his flat in Munich when I received my first letter from Kazz four years earlier. Wolfgang didn't really understand why I was putting so much effort into something so strange, but he sensed how important it was to me.

"You don't mind helping, do you? You always wanted to show me Berlin," I asked.

"It's just good to see you," he said.

A few hours from Hamburg, we stopped near the border between West and East Germany.

"We're only a few hours from Berlin," Wolfgang explained, "but we have to pass through East Germany. Once we're in East Germany, we can't really stop or get off the autobahn."

We filled the car with gas. At an ultramodern roadside café with brightly colored tables, we ordered chicken soup. The broth was rich, bursting with flavor. Wolfgang promised more food in Berlin, so we ate quickly and then jumped into the Mercedes to drive the short distance to the border control station. There a guard just glanced at Wolfgang's passport and stamped my American passport with an East German transit visa.

The long autumn sunset was turning dark as we drove deeper into the east. The well-lit billboards which had lined the highway from Hamburg disappeared. There were few road lights, and few signs of life beyond the crowded Trabants that moved slowly along the road. Wolfgang's twenty-year-old car roared past the miniature two-cycle East German automobiles.

Surrounded by all of this, our mood changed. It was as if the bleak scene outside were an unwanted guest sitting between us and casting darkness and gloom over us. I pulled my tape recorder from my bag and mocked a radio interview, trying for comic relief.

"Sitting next to me is a man by the name of Wolfgang Ettlich. It's exactly ten minutes to six. We are in East Germany en route to West Berlin. Ah, a sign! It says: *Berlin: der Haupstadt der DDR 159 km.* This man next to me—a very unusual German man, I might add, with a good sense of humor—was born in Berlin."

"That's right," Wolfgang said, answering me in English and getting into my playful game. "In 1947."

"That's him laughing there next to me. And in a minute we are going to ask him a few more questions. We want to know how he feels about going back to this lovely city in the middle of nowhere and..."

"Middle of nowhere?" he interrupted with mock indignation. "We're in the middle of the Cold War! Look! There is an enemy tank! No, I am wrong. It is just a truck. There is a nuclear warhead! No, it's just a farmhouse. But, there, that surely is the enemy on a dangerous mission." He laughed and then pointed to our left, where a dimly lit Trabant had turned off the main road and was headed out into the dark countryside.

"Okay, okay," I said. "So tell me what it was like growing up here in the middle of the not-so-visible enemy."

Wolfgang launched into a not-so-silly monologue about his life growing up in an ugly apartment surrounded by bombed-out buildings whose rubble prevented the children from playing anywhere but in the tiny backyard. He lived in Berlin's American-controlled section, and he vowed to go to America one day. When he finally did, he said, "The first thing they did in Times Square was rip me off."

A huge Mercedes truck, covered snugly with a blue tarp, roared passed us. I was suddenly curious about Wolfgang's father. The tape recorder made me bold.

"What did your father do during the war?"

"He was a mechanic. What about yours?"

For a moment I hesitated. My father had made illegal radios in Norway during World War II, and if the occupying German forces had found him out he would have been shot. Radios were lifelines to the outside world, and the Nazis wanted to cut the Norwegians off from all news except Nazi propaganda. When I told Wolfgang, he just nodded.

It was a chilling thought that our two fathers had once been at least technically enemies, but as we continued through the epicenter of the Cold War battleground, I envied them. Theirs was a tangible war. Carry a radio, or radio component, or break a rule and you were dead. Shot. Just like that. Wolfgang's and my war was full of ambiguities. It wasn't even a war. It was a "cold war," a war mostly in the minds of cool, calculating leaders. The actual fighting happened in proxy countries: in Central America, in Southeast Asia, and in Africa, but always with the same vagueness and ambiguity of purpose. Even the radiation that ultimately could kill all the Cold War participants was invisible. It killed slowly, horribly.

Wolfgang interrupted my thoughts, "Your father still work at the Lab?"

"He retired a few years ago," I said.

Ahead of us was a caravan of stopped trucks, with emergency lights flashing. Wolfgang gripped the steering wheel tighter and slowed the car.

Of course, my father had also experienced fear. He often told me that he had never been so scared as he was during World War II. It was fear, I'm sure, that drove him to work for the Lab, or at least gave him the justification for working there. He imagined he was helping ensure that nothing like the Nazi regime would ever happen again. It was fear that prompted him to build the bomb shelter. "The best offense," he would recite, "is a good defense."

But in this crazy modern world, his rational objective defenses didn't work. Bomb shelters, which were effective during earlier wars, seemed ultimately senseless in the face of a nuclear explosion. Ours became merely a backdrop for my childhood nightmares.

Even my father agreed that Star Wars—the ultimate rational defense—was a crazy idea. Perhaps that's why it was so important for him to help me place the first Shinto god in the lake in Norway. My father, unintentionally, had acknowledged that his ways weren't working. He didn't know if mine would, but he knew we had to stop this vicious cycle.

"Anyway," I said to Wolfgang after he had successfully navigated around the stopped trucks. "I'm conducting the interview. What about your father?"

Wolfgang continued talking about his father and his family. After a few moments, he seemed to have forgotten me and was only speaking for the microphone. "My father had no family. He didn't know his father, just his mother. He hated his stepfather. He was mostly raised by his grandmother. He left home when he was thirteen and joined Hitler's youth organization where he finally found a family and friends. He was happy."

Just before we entered Berlin, the wide, four-lane autobahn became a narrow, two-lane road. We passed a Soviet camp, with soldiers walking near the highway, guns slung over their shoulders. Wolfgang stopped talking.

At the West German checkpoint at West Berlin, the road broadened again. Running parallel to the road was the Berlin Wall, a concrete barrier illuminated with bright searchlights. We could see East German guards perched high above in towers. The Wall rose three times higher than a person could reach. It was capped with rusty barbed wire, and it seemed indestructible. I turned off the tape recorder, which had nearly reached the end of the tape anyway. Neither of us spoke until the road turned away and we were engulfed with the bright cheerful lights of West Berlin.

Wolfgang let out a long breath, which he had held when he first saw the Wall. "I love this city."

We stopped at a corner and picked up a few curry wursts and bread. It was Wolfgang's favorite kiosk, and the woman behind the counter recognized him even though he had moved to Munich many years earlier. She asked him about his film business, and he told her how happy he was to be in Berlin, if only for a few days.

We spent the night with friends of Wolfgang, in Kreuzberg, Wolfgang's old neighborhood, now filled pre-dominately with Turkish guest workers. While Wolfgang gossiped with his friends, I lay on the couch and listened to the BBC, then to American Armed Forces radio, and finally to the Voice of America before falling asleep.

For breakfast Wolfgang and I visited a Turkish coffeehouse and ordered tea, sipping the rich amber liquid from small clear glasses as we read the morning paper. Wolfgang read aloud a report about a bomb scare at a nearby hotel.

"That's nothing. Just a scare. It's calm. Things must be good between the United States and the Soviet Union, because Berlin is a barometer. Calm here means calm between the superpowers."

Just a few weeks earlier, President Reagan and the Soviet premier, Mikhail Gorbachev, had met in Reykjavík for a historic arms control summit. For a short time it looked as if they might agree to eliminate virtually all nuclear weapons. I was thrilled that once again my placing of a Shinto god had coincided with a move toward world peace. At the end of the summit, however, Gorbachev insisted that Star Wars be scrapped, and Reagan walked away from the negotiating table. Even though the superpowers had talked and the world seemed a little safer for it, I recalled the monster I had imagined on Lake Lögurinn and wondered if the calm was only short-lived.

Back in the car we began our tour of the neighborhood.

"I used to deliver mail here," said Wolfgang, pointing over the steering wheel. "I knew all the people. I loved the job."

"Here, this is where I was born," he said, motioning down a small street toward a lovely park filled with children playing. "This was all rubble."

Beyond the park was the Wall, looking a bit less dramatic than the night before, but still impressive.

I pulled out the tape recorder. This was historic, and I wanted him to tell me about the Wall and what he remembered.

Wolfgang hesitated for a moment. The tape recorder made him think carefully before answering.

"We lived very close to it. See."

He stopped the car so I could get a good look.

"It went up in July and August of 1961. I was fourteen, and away at summer camp. When they began to build it, my camp counselors told me that I could never go back to see my parents. They didn't know exactly where the Wall was placed. There was no way to phone so I couldn't call my mother. Finally I went back to Berlin. I think it was August 14th or 15th. The wall was only 200 meters from my house. We were still in the West, but I had friends on the other side. I immediately went looking for them. It was very crowded because everyone was looking for their friends and family. I never saw my friends again."

We got out of the car. I kept the tape recorder near Wolfgang as we walked toward the Wall.

"After a while it wasn't that big of a deal. The Wall became part of our playground. It belonged to my surroundings. We kicked the soccer ball against it. We painted it. It was quiet near the Wall since there weren't any cars. But I never understood why it was there.

"At first a lot of people escaped by jumping from the houses that were close to the Wall, but then they destroyed all the houses near the Wall and built the Wall higher.

"When I delivered mail, I used to throw cigarettes and newspapers over the Wall and talk with people. They asked me how it was over here. They asked if there was a possibility to open the Wall so they could see their children or friends. They didn't know what was going on because the government controlled the news.

"I don't like the Wall. I don't like that they forced people to join the party. But they have some good ideas in East

Germany. They have no unemployment. They have child care rights for the women. They have the same medical care for everyone.

"My friends call me a 'social romantic.' I just feel everything should be equal between people."

As we continued our tour of his old neighborhood, Wolfgang would periodically look at me and ask: "Here? Is this where you'd like to place the Shinto god?"

"No," I said. "Not yet."

We walked close to a canal that ran out from the Spree River. It was near the Wall, and an East German guard watched as we playfully took pictures of each other, our hands outstretched against the Wall.

Up close, the Wall no longer looked so indestructible. It was made of crummy concrete and there were many cracks. I reached into one and dislodged a piece the size of my fist. It was covered with blue graffiti.

I said to Wolfgang, "It'll make a good souvenir...."

Wolfgang looked at me patiently, wondering if I was joking.

Then he watched as I placed the piece of the Wall into my camera bag and pulled out the Shinto god. Before he could say anything, I unwrapped the cloth and turned my back toward the East German guard, perched high on the tower above us.

For a spilt second, I transported my mind back to 1961 when the world was sliding toward war. I thought of my father as he made plans to build the bomb shelter. I imagined nuclear warheads flying overhead. I saw Wolfgang and me as young boys. He had his Wall, and I had the walls of my bomb shelter, and we both wondered if we'd ever see past them to the light of the next day.

A group of ducks appeared on the river, and I tossed the stone god into the middle of the flock. The East German guard strained over the ledge trying to see what we were doing. I snapped a few pictures and handed the character-laden cloth to Wolfgang.

"It's yours. Now you have a souvenir too," I said to my friend.

The placing had come easily, much like the first time in Norway: no angst, no doubts, and no strange happenings. I had put into motion the promise I had made to myself in New York. The last two placings had come much more easily since I had fully committed myself to the project.

chapter 16

The Baltic Sea ferry boat en route
to Finland.

Each individual who conquers the panic of their nightmare, who
faces up to the terror of evil, and thereby discovers a goodness
which heals and cannot be destroyed, brings fresh love into the
world. The deepening of their capacity for love will first heal their
own wound, and then go further, spreading its gentle influence
upon family and friends.

—*Nightmares in Human Conflict,* by John Mack

A day after I placed the god in Berlin, Wolfgang drove me to
the West Berlin train station. I planned to head north by
night train to Norway, briefly visit my relatives, then continue by train to Stockholm. From there, I would take a ferry
to Finland. My plan was to place a god in the Baltic Sea during the crossing.

Shortly after the train left West Berlin, it ground to a halt on the other side of the Wall inside the East Berlin station, which was dimly lit and smelled of burnt coal. Big guard dogs, black ears pointed to the sky, patrolled the tracks, their masters looking every bit as serious. My fear of borders was instantly awakened. Stoic passport control officers looked very carefully at every page of my passport, but the baggage check was perfunctory and the second god remained undisturbed. I settled nervously into my sleeping couchette and finally fell asleep to the gentle swaying of the train as it slowly moved north through the dark countryside.

It was still dark outside when I woke in a panic. The nightmare had returned. As usual, it involved me, the bomb shelter, and the evil. I couldn't see the evil but as usual it pounded on the escape hatch door, taunting me to open it. The only thing between me and the outside was the escape hatch door and the evil, and I was frozen with fear. This time, however, like in my nightmare in New York, I actually reached for the door. This time I heard Kazz behind me softly telling me to open it. I cracked the door open, and the pounding on the other side suddenly stopped. The silence terrified me, and I quickly shut the door and froze, unable to move. Kazz disappeared and I woke, drenched in sweat.

Damn, I thought, things are going so well. Why did it come back now? As I woke more completely, I realized that my nightmare had fundamentally changed from the days when I could do nothing but freeze in terror in front of the escape hatch door. Instead of blaming the Sword of Heaven project for bringing my nightmare back to the surface, I now suspected the project was helping me work through the nightmare. With that thought, I rolled over and went back to sleep.

The next morning the Danish border check was virtually nonexistent; several hours later the Swedish guards were more thorough, but they were looking for illegal amounts of liquor and drugs and didn't seem concerned with the heavy package in my suitcase. Late that afternoon, there were no checks at the Norwegian border—a surprise considering a story Kazz had told me about placing the god in Spitsbergen, high above the Arctic Circle.

He had booked passage on a ship from England that stopped in Bergen, Norway, before continuing north. The god was contained in a much larger than normal stone, packed especially for the North Pole, which Kazz's teacher considered a very powerful place. The Norwegian border guards wanted to open the package and see its contents. Kazz protested, explaining it was a sacred object and that there could be real trouble if it were opened. The Norwegians were firm, and Kazz finally agreed on the condition that there be a special ceremony. He pulled a white robe from his luggage, donned it and kneeled in the custom area. Pressing his hands together he started chanting and praying. Embarrassed by this outpouring of emotion and religious devotion, the Norwegian guards stuffed the huge god into Kazz's bag and sent Kazz through with no further delay.

Four years had passed since I placed the first Shinto god in the lake near my family home. My father was back in California so I stayed with my aunt and uncle. My schedule was so tight and the fall weather so bad that I didn't visit the lake where I had placed the god, but I did go to see my 70-year-old great aunt, who owned the cabin there. We talked about the family, the weather, and the rest home where she received such good care, and then we easily slipped into a conversation about the Shinto project. She knew about the first placing and wondered how the project was going. She had read about many peace projects in the Norwegian press. "Was this one of them?" she wondered. "Probably not," I said. "It's not your average peace project." No, she hadn't heard of any children diving in the lake after the god. Then we continued our conversation about family and friends, and I left not thinking for a moment that it was strange to talk about Shinto gods with my elderly relative. I had come a long way since I first told my father about the project, when even the word "god" had stuck in my throat.

Ten years earlier when I was living in Helsinki researching material for a book on sweat bathing customs around the world, I grew to love crossing Norway and Sweden by night train, then connecting to a ship for the crossing to Helsinki. The trip takes two full nights, and the boat ride across the Baltic Sea is my favorite part of the journey. My plan to place a Shinto god only slightly varied my routine.

I arrived at the Stockholm harbor at 4:30 p.m. I had spent the day in Stockholm, as I usually did, visiting museums in the old town and enjoying a quaint coffee shop near the train station. The boat departed at 6 p.m. so I headed to my bunk in a small but comfortable cabin. The cabin had a shower, but instead I headed to the bottom of the ship where I joined a group of Finns with a similar mission: a real Finnish sauna. It's here that I always experience culture shock. Being surrounded by Norwegians and Swedes is familiar to me. But the Finns! The language is so strange. Even the word for "telephone," a recognizable word around the world, is alien: *puhen*. Photography? The Finns say *valokuva*.

The ship was full of reminders that I was headed into a different land. There were two clocks, one with Swedish time and the other with Finnish time, an hour later; two currencies, Finnish markka and Swedish krona; two languages; and two distinct types of people. In the sauna, the boisterous Finns yelled and cried in their strange tongue as they splashed water on the sizzling rocks. They were happy to be almost home. The Swedes were invariably silent.

After the sauna I went back to my room to dress for dinner. I had dreamed of the smorgasbord all day: piles of salmon, roast game, Finnish black bread, caviar, potatoes and fresh country vegetables, pickled herring, and generous amounts of dairy-rich desserts.

My normal after-dinner routine on the overnight boat was to go upstairs to hear live music and play roulette and blackjack. But this night I went out on deck, where it was raining. I was alone except for a couple kissing near a lifeboat. Their faces melted into each other, like an Edvard Munch painting, so all I saw were two bodies and one head. I thought of Donna.

We'd shared so much: my confusion in Japan, my malaise upon returning to San Francisco, my terror about the tornado in Florida, and, of course, New York. Through it all she had suffered my debilitating ambivalence. How many times had she pleaded, "What do you want?" She could have been asking about the Shinto project, or about us: for both I only offered vague answers. In New York, with my back against the wall, I had finally made the choice to cast aside the last of my doubts and finish the project.

Why couldn't I cast aside my doubts about Donna? I felt I carried a heavy burden, and suddenly I thought of my bomb shelter nightmare. My inability to resolve Donna felt connected to my inability to resolve the nightmare.

Until I resolved my nightmare, until I made it through the door and confronted the evil, it would continue to darken

my heart and keep me from fully engaging in life. It would
keep me from fully loving Donna or anyone who tried to get
close to me. I was getting closer, I knew that. But would I
figure it out in time for Donna and me?

I stood on the stern of the boat and watched the lights of
the coast and waited for the ferry to pass the last of the
coastal islands and reach the open sea. When the ship began
tossing on the high seas and the lights disappeared, I heaved
the god overboard. In the powerful wake of the ship, I didn't
see the splash. The rain came down harder. The couple
stopped kissing and gently pushed away from each other.

chapter 17

Placing the god in Puerto Rico.

"I know the ending.

One day it will happen.

One day we will see flashes, all of us.

One day my daughter will die. One day, I know, my wife will leave me. It will be autumn, perhaps, and the trees will be in color, and she will kiss me in my sleep and tuck a poem in my pocket, and the world will surely end."

—*The Nuclear Age*, by Tim O'Brien

In February 1987, three months after I returned from Europe, *Parenting* magazine called to ask for pictures of children playing in the sun. Hawaii was out, the photo editor said, they'd just published a piece from there. Did I have any other suggestions?

I knew that a god had been placed in the Panama Canal but none in the Caribbean. I suggested Puerto Rico, but the magazine balked: too expensive, my editor said. But the Hyatt Hotel at Cerromar Beach agreed to provide airfare from New York to San Juan and accommodations if they were credited as the location for the shoot. *Parenting* would only have to get me to New York. The trip was on.

When I called Donna, she was thrilled at the thought of escaping New York's winter cold. She would come along as my assistant.

When all the details were worked out, I was filled with accomplishment and anticipation. I had found a place for another god, a way for me and Donna to spend time together, and I would be paid for it all! The Sword of Heaven project was truly inspired. See what happens when you make up your mind? I could do no wrong. My ego soared as my plane took off for New York to pick up Donna.

The first sign that something was wrong came at the airport in San Juan, where I had been assured by the public relations agency that the sun shines 90 percent of the time. It was raining.

"Unusual weather," said the porter with a shrug as he lifted my camera equipment into the hotel van.

"Yeah, I don't need children playing in the rain. This better clear up."

The hotel was fantastic, with tiled floors and a bed the size of a New York studio apartment. There was a well-stocked refrigerator and a small porch facing the nearby beach. But it rained the second day and the third day and the fourth. When it stopped and the sun burst through the clouds, we rushed to the beach along with the rest of the guests. But by the afternoon it was raining again, and I only had a dozen or so mediocre shots of children in the sun.

I was angry and Donna was depressed.

We had hoped the trip would give us time to solve our unsatisfying living situation and clarify our relationship. The rain was ominous.

Trying to snap the mood, we rented a car and drove to the eastern tip of the island, where we boarded a ferry to Vieques Island. The rains had caused flooding, and the boat was thrown violently around. We passed the skeleton of an earlier ferry, recently capsized in the stormy sea.

Still searching, we checked into a hotel which was advertised as a "beach club." It was a mile from the beach, and our room was in shambles. The hot water didn't work. The bed was wrapped in plastic with only a thin polyester sheet to cover it. The windows didn't close and the door wouldn't lock. The hotel restaurant made TV dinners look like gourmet dining. In the middle of the night, my pillow burst, and I woke almost suffocated from the foam rubber pieces.

The next night we tried another place, a stately old mansion converted into a hotel. The calm scene was suddenly broken by the cry of one of the guests: someone had stolen $500 in cash he was keeping in his room. The owner scurried around, trying to reassure everyone, but it was obviously an inside job by one of the employees. Everyone was on edge.

"Can't anything go right?" I said to Donna.

She had a plan. She had been sitting beside the tiny pool in the courtyard next to a young couple from Boston. They had rented a jeep and knew of a beach nearby where they planned to spend the day. Did we want to join them?

Playa Azul is official navy territory, closed to the public during maneuvers, but open the rest of the time. Our only company on the beach was a navy man, dressed in fatigues, jogging toward us on the dirt road, his hairy chest dripping with sweat.

I immediately took the Shinto god from my pack and walked alone a half mile to where the sandy beach turned into a rocky one. I jumped into the water, carrying the god. Not more than a hundred yards from the rocks, I noticed a huge head of waving coral, which reminded me of Hanukkah candles. I dove, placed the god snugly into the head of coral and surfaced. For a long time I floated and thought about Donna and me.

"This isn't working. She's not happy. I'm not happy."

Like tiny bubbles coming off the ocean bottom, my thoughts started slowly, with few reaching the surface. But the longer I floated, the more powerful they became.

I loved her, yes. But we'd allowed 3,000 miles to come between us. Was that love?

When the Shinto teacher had spoken of love (after saying Donna and I were like brother and sister), he spoke of the love of Christ, the universal love. I had no trouble understanding that concept. It made sense: we have to live together on this small planet or we will perish. But the love between a man and a woman, specifically between me and Donna, that was different. That I didn't understand.

I knew I didn't want to go to New York. But couldn't she come back to San Francisco? What if she says no? What if she says yes? Both possibilities frightened me.

What's wrong with you? I berated myself. Are you scared to ask her for what you want?

I rose and fell with the swells, listening to the pounding of my heart. After a moment it seemed to beat in synch with the pulsing ocean.

Okay, okay! I *am* scared, I thought. Scared of being consumed. Scared of her powerful sense of self. Her confidence. Her determination. I'm also scared of losing myself.

There are books written about men like me. We should be required to wear tags: "Beware, man scared of intimacy!"

Mothers should warn their daughters: "Watch out for the shy, sensitive types. They make good friends but…"

Finally, I swam back to the beach still feeling unresolved about Donna, but sensing that something was going to change, something I didn't have the power to stop.

It was still raining when we returned to San Juan, so we cut our trip short and flew back to New York. Donna and I said goodbye. I was flying back to San Francisco. She handed me the overcoat that I usually kept at her apartment, and the finality of it came crashing down on me. She looked at me sadly, then turned back to her apartment. I got in the taxi and cried on the way to the airport. Fear had won.

I wasn't surprised when the pictures of children in the sun were rejected. The images are too dull, the magazine's art director said.

chapter 18

My classmates and me at the
Iwakiyama monastery.

*In the fall of 1987, the world was on the brink of peace. The
failed summit between Reagan and Gorbachev in Iceland had set
the stage for a series of talks that led to the historic Intermediate-
Range Nuclear Forces (INF) Treaty, which for the first time
reduced the total number of nuclear warheads. Later, when
Gorbachev was asked what he thought was the turning point in
U.S.-USSR relations, he didn't hesitate. "Reykjavík," he said.
"Because for the first time the two leaders talked directly over an
extended period in a real conversation about key issues."*

    *It turns out that the monster I saw on Lake Lögurinn was
not a sign of the end after all, but of the beginning.*

Kazz wrote me in October of 1987 and told me that most of
the gods had been placed. Only a few more placings were
needed. He acknowledged that the world situation had indeed improved, but the time before completion was the most
precarious and dangerous time of all. The fire ceremony, an
ancient annual rite Kazz said was the most important Shinto
ceremony, would take place on the 13th of November at
Iwakiyama monastery. During the ceremony, a huge battle for
world peace would be waged, and all the gods that we had
placed around the world would be called upon to protect the
earth during this especially critical time.

On November 8th I boarded the train in Tokyo at
9 a.m., heading south toward Iwakiyama, the same monastery where the teacher had promised me special training in
the ways of Shinto.

Not only was I looking forward to this trip as closure to
a confusing but ultimately rewarding five years, but I had also
taken the teacher's promise of special training to heart. I
hoped the training would give me the power he had said I
was lacking during my first visit to Japan.

Kazz hopped on the train in Osaka a few hours later,
wearing a formal three-piece suit. I had only seen him
dressed casually or in Shinto robes, and I teased him about
looking like a businessman. "Bought in Turkey for $70," Kazz
said proudly, tugging on the vest as he sat down next to me
and the train continued south.

He seemed more relaxed than on my previous visits. He

had put on weight, which actually flattered him. We talked about cameras and computers, and it was a while before we turned to the Sword of Heaven.

I gave him details about the placings in Iceland, Berlin, and the Baltic Sea. "These placings were easy compared to Florida and the Philippines. However," I added, "Puerto Rico was difficult for a different reason. Donna and I…"

Kazz waited.

"We broke up," I said finally.

He looked disappointed. "I'm sorry."

As the bullet train sped south, Kazz explained that we would spend the next four days in classes and in preparation for the ceremony. He also said that on Friday night I would be the first Westerner to witness the fire ceremony.

"What about Juan?" I asked.

Kazz shook his head.

I hadn't seen Juan Li for over a year but through letters and an occasional phone call I knew he had found his calling. He was studying Tai Chi, a Chinese martial art, on the East Coast with a famous teacher named Mantak Chia. Juan hoped to become a Tai Chi teacher himself one day.

I asked where Takizawa the teacher was, and how he was doing.

"He's fine. He's still in Osaka," Kazz answered. "He will arrive at the end of the week, in time for the ceremony."

"In the meantime, who will conduct the classes, who will teach me the Shinto ways?" I asked.

"The other teachers."

"Others?"

"I told you. Hakuryu Takizawa is just one of several disciples of Tomokiyo, the founder of the monastery."

I remembered that Takizawa was also keeping the Sword of Heaven project secret from them. Why?

"Actually, he told them about the project a year ago," Kazz said in response to my question. "He even wrote a book about the project."

A book? This was the first I had heard of a book.

"He published it himself and printed a few hundred copies. He gave the other teachers copies and they were very upset. They asked him to put the book away and not to sell or give away any more copies."

"Were they angry?"

"No, but they didn't like that he had kept it a secret from them. I also don't think they understood what he is trying to do."

"But he's still part of the group? He's still welcome at the monastery?"

"Oh yes, there is no problem."

This time I didn't even try to understand.

We both fell asleep, and woke just before our arrival

in Hiroshima, where we were required to change to a local train.

It was my second visit to this tragic city, but I expect that my reaction would have been the same had it been my twentieth: horror at how far humans will go to destroy each other.

Today things look normal. Nearly all of the city has been rebuilt since that August day in 1945 when 90 percent of the town was destroyed by the atomic bomb dubbed "Little Boy." It was a military action, carefully planned and ostensibly executed to end World War II, but I imagine that to the people on the ground it must have seemed like the apocalypse itself, an instant judgment by a faceless god.

At the epicenter of the blast stands a memorial called Peace City. The original city hall—which was only partially destroyed—is now a museum exhibiting pieces of sidewalk etched with the shadows of people standing there at the time of the blast. The first time I visited, there was also an exhibit of drawings by adults who were children when the blast occurred. The horrific drawings were done as therapy, an attempt to exorcise the terror their creators couldn't forget. Many contained bodies melting under rays of light; pieces of arms, legs, and heads, floating in rivers red with blood; and blackened eyes looking pleadingly to the sky. The mushroom cloud was ever-present, and in many of the drawings it actually looked beautiful.

I felt a part of Hiroshima lived inside me, not only

because I was a citizen of the country that dropped the bomb but because I was part of the bomb's legacy. My father had worked at a nuclear weapons lab whose aim was to develop bigger and more powerful weapons of mass destruction. The weapons created by the Livermore Lab made the bomb dropped on Hiroshima seem tiny by comparison.

Kazz and I ate lunch at a station noodle shop and then went to a nearby grocery store to buy dried fruit, nuts, cheese, and orange juice for the rest of our journey.

We boarded a local train full of schoolchildren, all healthy and full of laughter. The train stopped frequently on its slow trip along the coast and passed the famous Miyajima shrine that rose gracefully from the sea before reaching the small town of Tabuse. There we hailed a taxi to take us to the monastery at the base of Iwakiyama.

As we drove toward the monastery, Kazz explained that when Tomokiyo founded the monastery, he believed that all the ancient Shinto knowledge should be kept there and that in case of an apocalypse, it would become a sort of *fune* or ark, that would preserve all knowledge.

I was thinking that his description of the mountain retreat was very much like Shangri-la, the mythical country tucked in the Himalayan mountains, far from the dangers of the world. But then I remembered that we were only a few hours from Hiroshima, and it occurred to me that in the real world there is no safe place.

"Did the blast reach this far?" I asked.

"They heard the explosion," answered Kazz. "In fact, one of the teachers at Iwakiyama made the mistake of going into Hiroshima two hours after the blast. He has had medical trouble ever since. He never had children."

The taxi left us at the base of the mountain, in front of a cluster of one- and two-story buildings. Kazz introduced me to the monastery's administrator and three teachers who happened by. At the office I filled out papers that I could not read with my name and address. Kazz paid for my room and lodging, explaining that Takizawa was my benefactor. I reached for my wallet and protested, but this time Kazz was insistent and because no actual cash changed hands, I felt okay about accepting the generous gift.

After we completed the paperwork, we walked outside, where we were surrounded by deciduous trees in their full fall glory. Behind the office were two large auditoriums filled with tatami mats. This was where we'd sleep and attend classes.

"And up there," said Kazz as he pointed up the hill to a large building with a high arching ceiling of wood, "is one of the many shrines on the mountain. And beyond it, farther up the mountain, near the summit, is our most important shrine. We call it *Yamato-Jinjya*, and it represents the center of the spiritual world on this earth. That's where we will hold the fire ceremony at the end of the week, on Friday."

As we strolled around the monastery compound, Kazz explained that starting tomorrow, Monday, we'd purify our bodies in preparation for Friday's fire ceremony. We were required to eat only *Kessai* food, which meant no chemicals, nothing powdered (including tofu), no eggs, no miso, and no meat, leaving mainly rice and vegetables. There was to be no talking between the students, but Kazz had received special permission to translate the lessons for me.

That night after a last "normal" dinner of tofu, cabbage, green tea, and a nectarine for dessert, I was introduced to the other participants. Some had come from as far away as Hokkaido, the northernmost island. I recognized a few from the ceremonies I attended during my earlier trips to Japan. They were happy to see me. In his enthusiasm, one chubby man from Osaka bashed his bowed head into mine. We patted each other's hair and laughed.

Before going to bed, I was given a two-piece kimono. One piece was skirtlike and the other like a large shirt. After I put them on, I made the mistake of looking at myself in a mirror. I looked absurdly tall and awkward. I quickly turned away.

I was also given an amulet to wear around my neck. There was one vertical bar with an emblem of the shrine set in relief in the middle. Out from the axis was a single bar running to the left. Farther down was another bar running right.

If the two side pieces were slid to meet one another, it would look like a Christian cross.

"The disjointed side bars are in the process of coming together," Kazz told me as he hung the medallion over my head. "It's this process—the act of becoming—that Shinto is primarily concerned with, not so much with being."

For the next four days, we awoke at dawn to begin the day with a short chanting ceremony at the shrine near the auditoriums. Then we breakfasted on the specially prepared food, which tasted bland but was edible. Classes started promptly after breakfast and lasted until lunch, with one mid-morning break. We had the afternoons free to do what we wanted. In the evenings we prayed and chanted at a nearby shrine.

Although there were hints of the ascetic in our strict diet and vow of silence, Kazz told me that denial is not for a Shintoist. "The teacher says not to bother being a puritanical saint. The *kami* way is free, easy, rich, and grand. If you weaken your body with too much discipline, you leave it open for bad spirits. If you suffer for enlightenment, you come to love emptiness."

We certainly didn't suffer. At night, after a busy day, we sat in Japanese baths, soaking quietly. The hot water relaxed my stiff legs and knees, which were unfamiliar with the long squatting and kneeling. Except for one night when I had a disturbing dream about Donna and a motorcycle accident, I slept well. Students who snored were quickly given a room alone. We certainly were not fasting. I was surrounded by considerate and polite people. It didn't rain. It wasn't too cold, and the fall leaves were beautiful.

The classes were different each of the four days. Some of the subjects could have come from the front pages of a supermarket tabloid—soul stabilization, astral travel, extra-sensory perception, and spirit possession. Others were simply practical and offered ways to relax and enjoy the world around us.

At first, I participated in the classes with the detachment of a journalist. I dutifully took notes and at the same time withdrew into a familiar space where the content slid by me without sticking. It was the same space I'd frequent when I was with Donna, and it would drive her crazy as she tried to figure out where I'd gone.

After just one day, however, I saw the effect the classes were having on my classmates. At the end of a day of classes and prayer, I saw my fellow students walk with their shoulders thrust proudly back, their hearts easily exposed, radiating self-confidence. I became convinced that these people would return to their jobs as business people, lawyers, and factory workers knowing that their thoughts and actions were important, that they did make a difference in an inherently benevolent world.

I thought of my own culture, where the mind is treated separately from the body, where the observer is always separate from the observed, where God is separate from Nature, and I found something profoundly unsettling about the model I was raised with. The ability to stand back and observe is the essence of science but at what price do we do so? In my own experience disengagement is always followed by sadness and loneliness and a sense of impotency. There was definitely a lesson here to be learned, and I began to open up and really accept what I was hearing.

"Shinto means 'Way of the Gods' in Japanese," Kazz said quietly during one of the first classes. "Other religions *explain* the way, while Shinto *shows* the way to power."

On the second day, after classes were over, I found a small pond with a red torii placed in the middle. The spot was in a secluded ravine, high up the mountain. I stood at the water's edge, surrounded by trees and brush, staring at the simple shrine. I clapped my hands, just as I had seen Kazz do many times. The clapping called the attention of the gods.

"Sound is the most pure of all matter in the world," Kazz had told me that morning during a class on *Oto-dama*, or sound purification. "All beings are moved by the cosmic vibration. Even Amaterasu-Omikami, the Sun Goddess, was lured from her cave by the sound of dancing and laughing. We are all connected by sound vibrations. We become one with the sound."

The teacher of the class had told us to take fifteen minutes or more each day to sit comfortably and listen closely to a fixed sound of a clock or a metronome, a waterfall or a sea wave, a little stream, or even an insect. "Don't try and stop your mind, because then it will do the opposite!" he had explained. "Just listen, that's all."

I listened as the sound of my clapping echoed back to me. I prayed, just repeating the Sun Goddess's name over and over, finding pleasure in the sound.

A distorted duplicate of the red shrine was reflected in the water. A burst of wind blew ripples on the surface, rustling the bushes and disturbing a bird which flew into the blue sky and disappeared in a burst of bright light. I felt power, pleasure, and reverence. I couldn't remember a single church or a cathedral that had evoked such wonder in me as that simple Shinto shrine.

The next afternoon I returned to my secluded spot. I had just attended a morning class on *Yusai*, spirit possession. Even though in New York I had decided not to get hung up on the question of spirits, an entire morning on the subject had put my rational mind into full gear, and I struggled once again to make sense of it all.

"There are three types of spirit possession of the soul," Kazz translated while the very serious teacher explained. "*Shinkan* is considered the highest possession. It comes directly from the highest God to man. It is subtle, and one is never aware of the possession until much later.

"*Jikan* is possession by one god or another without the use of a medium.

"*Takan* is possession with a medium. *Takan* is the most dramatic form of possession. It's very dangerous. Often mere animal spirits or unenlightened spirits take possession of a person. Sometimes what is thought of as a spirit possession is nothing more than an overactive nervous system.

"Don't be fooled by these lowly spirits. They are very mischievous. They can lift a sword in the air, or emanate a light, but the clever spirits are just using *your* energy to do this."

Kazz had tried to explain. "The relationship between the spirit world and man is like that of a television and a broadcast station. You have to be careful what channel you switch to. A little self-conceit or egotism switches you immediately to a black *kami* channel. Its shadow then covers the golden light of the white *kami*."

I was comfortable with the world of hard objects, the world of things that can be touched and quantified, the world of my father. I became a photojournalist which, like science, observes and reports on events and life. It is considered an ethical lapse when a journalist participates or engages in an event, even though journalists do it all the time.

Kazz and the other students saw beyond the material world to a place full of dynamic and changing forces that dance to a rhythm beyond my comprehension, yet something was driving me toward that world. Something in me wanted very much to accept and embrace that world, bad spirits and all. I wouldn't have gotten so involved with the Sword of Heaven otherwise. I also saw that my need for a rational explanation was the very thing that was keeping me from getting there. To modify Kazz's metaphor, I was stuck on the Science channel, and I needed to switch to the Shinto channel.

Suddenly, after several minutes of staring at the beautiful shrine, a small dove dived from a nearby tree and nearly grazed my shoulder. At first I was startled, but then a warm glow started in my stomach and spread throughout my body. I sat down and sobbed.

When I looked up a few minutes later, I saw a leaf blown by a soft wind drop gently onto the water's surface. First there was one ripple, then another and another moving out from the leaf. I remembered the ripples in Norway when I placed the god with my father.

At that moment I made peace with my father and the world he had passed on to me. I saw myself as an outer ripple in a continuum of ever-expanding circles. As I moved farther from the center, I could now encompass his world as well as the world of Shinto. In this new world, I decided, the spirits are welcome.

Early Wednesday morning I ran into Kazz in the rest room. He had splashed water on his face and looked pale and drawn. I motioned him outside where we could talk without anyone seeing us. I asked him what was wrong. He paused and then told me he hadn't slept much. He had had a nightmare.

"A demon with a bird face came after me," he said. "I tried to get rid of him by using some of the techniques I learned yesterday, but they didn't work. Then God talked to me directly. The demon heard the voice of God and got scared and broke into many pieces."

Although Kazz was upset about his inability to use traditional Shinto techniques in his dream, it was clear to me that he had found his own power. I told him so, and I could see by his expression that he hadn't considered this.

"Perhaps your power is different from what they teach here, because Takizawa is different."

At the mention of his teacher, Kazz's face brightened.

"He is very special. There is no one here like him."

As we walked toward the classroom, Kazz clearly seemed better. My thoughts turned fondly toward Takizawa. His meeting with Jesus Christ had opened his heart to a world beyond his own, and he had combined the idea of the great love for all of mankind with the ancient and powerful spiritual belief of Shinto to come up with the Sword of Heaven. I felt that in that single act he took Shinto from an important, yet narrowly focused belief, into a world-class religion, one that could really make a difference. I was honored to be a small part of it.

The class that morning was on *Chinkon-Ho*, or soul stabilization. It was explained to us as a method of fixing the soul to the center of the body. Like *Oto-dama,* I saw in *Chinkon-Ho* a special way to bring the mind and body together and further open myself to the world.

During a twenty-minute break between morning sessions, I tried *Chinkon-Ho* at a makeshift desk I had set up near a window to write. I used a special stone that Kazz lent me. It was small and round, and he had found it in a mountain stream. He kept it in a soft fabric bag and washed it frequently. Even though he lent it to me, he said it should never be shown to others.

I did as I was told and sat upright in front of the stone which lay on the top of my desk. Down the hall I could see other students using the break to do the same. I positioned my fingers and hands carefully so that the first fingers of each hand stood straight up and the tips touched. I placed my left thumb softly across the right one while my other fingers were crossed inside the palm. I closed my eyes and concentrated on the stone.

I was silent, but I heard the other students chanting the special prayer the teacher had told us to chant: *Hito-Futa-Mi-Yo-Itsu-Muyu-Nana-Ya-Koko-No-To.*

The chant was simply counting from one to ten in Japanese. It is supposed to evoke the moments surrounding the creation of the Universe.

As I sat there concentrating on the stone, I felt myself absorbed in its essence. All my disparate parts—my body, my mind, my soul—went into the stone and became one with it. I stared back at it with an empty mind. I became aware of my breathing, which connected me with each inhalation to the stone and thereby to myself. For a second I sensed Creation itself, the moment when all matter came from the nothingness, and I relaxed.

After the break, we returned to a class that described the Shinto pantheon in detail. The teacher for this subject was a kindly, elderly man who was renowned for his skill as an archer. He explained that at the center of the pantheon is the supreme *kami* —Ameno-Minakanushi-no-kami—a force so sacred and mysterious it lives well beyond our normal senses. It is too subtle to manifest itself, and is said to live in a heavenly world situated near the North Star. It seemed to me that this God was very much like the biblical one: omniscient and omnipotent.

A Shintoist, however, doesn't limit the universe to only one God. The second in command is Amaterasu-Omikami, the Sun Goddess, who is the direct ruler of the solar system. She has the divine world inside and a fire outside. The emperor is believed to be a direct descendant of the Sun Goddess.

Under her there arc 181 classes of *kami*, and each *kami* has its own name, character, and world. Each has discrete abilities and power. For example, Okuninushi-no-kami rules the earth and judges where a person goes after death. Its up to this *kami* to determine if a person goes on to be part of another *kami*, or a part of something of little value, or simply to be reborn as a human again.

Furthermore, he explained, the astral world is divided into a white *kami* world and a black *kami* world. He explained that evil as a fixed or constant entity as we know it in the West doesn't exist in Shinto. The white or good *kami* are pure, inspire noble deeds, and make a person happy and rich. Black or bad *kami* are simply impure, and black *kami* can also bring luck or healing. Nothing is fixed or dogmatic. The gods, like humans, have free will.

The higher the spirit is in the pantheon of gods, the more information or knowledge it has, as well as power. It is therefore important to choose carefully to which god a question should be addressed.

"After all, you wouldn't bother a high god with a simple question that could very well be answered by a lower spirit," the teacher said.

I really liked one of the last things the teacher said before the class ended. "The *kami* world is very busy. The gods help men of wisdom and courage, but it is often better to do something by ourselves, without asking for help."

The final lesson was about ancestor worship. "All evil comes when ancestors are forgotten," explained our teacher, the one who had entered Hiroshima after the bomb was dropped.

He went on to say that all our strength, weakness, and courage come from those who passed before us and gave us life. If proper funeral and memorial rites are not performed for a dead person, it is believed that the dead spirit will wander through the human world and haunt people. Only special rituals, which were described but not taught, could correct this condition.

"Think of the family lineage as a river," he said finally. "Clean water travels downstream. But if someone upstream pollutes the water then somewhere along the way someone must do the cleaning."

He explained that there were many different ways for this cleansing to take place. But always, when the cleaning first starts bad things happen. Their severity depends on how polluted the river has become. The more pollution, the more difficult the cleaning.

As he went on to describe various purification rituals, it occurred to me that the Sword of Heaven project was one huge purification ritual for the earth. It also occurred to me that the project was a way for me to both honor those before me and perhaps make things easier for those to come.

chapter 19

The teacher speaking to us on the
morning of the Fire Ceremony.

*"This religious nuclear-age story is far from over. It may be that
spiritual response to Hiroshima is just now beginning."*

—*Hiroshima in America, A Half Century of Denial,* by Robert Jay Lifton & Greg Mitchell

On the morning of the fire ceremony, Hakuryu Takizawa,
the White Dragon, arrived from Osaka accompanied by
several of his congregation. They had prepared for the
ceremony on their own, adhering to the special diet and
praying.

I didn't notice any tension between him and the other
teachers, but soon after he arrived the group from Osaka,
including me and a few of my classmates, found a room in
one of the smaller buildings and spent the morning gathered

around our teacher, apart from the others. Our vow of silence was over and the room was full of happy conversation.

The first thing the teacher said when he saw me was, "You look younger!" Kazz, as usual, translated.

Then the teacher asked me how the classes had gone.

"Really well," I answered, mindful that he had paid for my week at the monastery. "I especially liked the classes on *Oto-dama* and *Chinkon-Ho*. They helped me relax, and, yes, they made me feel younger."

The teacher then asked me if I had found my power.

I didn't answer quickly. I had opened up to the spirit world, I had learned to bring my mind and body together, I had relaxed. But I knew something was missing, and I hadn't pulled everything together yet.

"I'm getting there," I said smiling.

My answer seemed to satisfy him, and he turned back to the others, giving them final words of advice for the evening ceremony.

"Be careful of your state of mind!" he said. "The astral world is like a mirror making an instant reflection on this side. To be a spiritual soldier for good, the mind must be pure and strong."

At noon of that day we assembled in the courtyard. There were about a hundred of us, and we took a group picture. Four wooden boxes of different sizes and shapes containing sacred objects were transferred carefully from the large shrine at the compound. Then a procession began at a smaller shrine near our classroom. We walked single file. The mountain was steep but the path that we followed was winding and gradual. We walked slowly and no one lagged behind. Every 30 minutes or so the packages were ritualistically passed between masked bearers.

Several hours later, at the top of the mountain, we rested. A light supper was served, and we adjusted our kimonos for the final ceremony. We wrapped a narrow piece of cloth over our shoulders and across our chests, making an X in the back. Everyone, including me, covered the tops of their heads with a white headband. Some of the men took out their long samurai-like swords. I had only the small dagger, the replica of the original Sword of Heaven that Kazz had given me a few years earlier. The rest of the people carried a leafy branch called *tamagushi*. "The *tamagushi* becomes a sword," Kazz said. "It is used just like the sword to push away bad spirits. We push them away, not cut them. We don't want them to become two. After the ceremony the *tamagushi* is offered to the fire."

One by one we filed into a small clearing in the woods near the main shrine. The night sky was filled with stars. Someone used a spark to ignite a large fire in the middle of the clearing, and as the fire consumed the stacks of wood the people around me softly chanted. One of the participants pounded slowly on a huge wooden drum that was strapped to his chest. The sound reminded me of a pulsing heart. The wooden boxes containing the sacred objects which had been so carefully carried up the mountain were paraded around the fire. Bamboo was tossed on the fire, which crackled and spit like an angry serpent. A woman stood in the middle of the circle and read from a scroll. I recognized Japanese words such as stone, gate, and open, and I understood she was asking the gods to let us in. The fire glowed on everyone's faces, and I could tell they looked as though they were slipping into a deep trance. I pulled out my camera, knowing I needed something to remind me that this was really happening. After I snapped a few frames, I put the camera down. I didn't want picture taking to interfere with my experiencing the ceremony.

On cue from the ceremony leaders, the participants began chanting archaic Japanese words. Then, as in Osaka, they began swinging their swords and leafy branches in front of them. I looked over and saw that Takizawa had no sword or *tamagushi*. He was waving his hands and arms. I turned my head and saw Kazz waving his huge sword, oblivious to my stare. After a few moments, I raised my dagger and began waving it and chanting as deliberately as everyone else around me.

I had no idea how long the ceremony lasted. I felt time had become elastic. Although it was past midnight, I felt no fatigue. Finally, after several loads of wood burned down to embers, we stopped chanting, and one of the teachers began to speak. Kazz didn't translate, leaving me with no idea what the teacher was saying. Takizawa was silent, and I wondered what he was thinking. After the speech was over, we slowly walked the short distance to the nearby shrine. There was a brief ceremony, which included chugging a cup of sake, and then we walked in the dark down the steep road toward the school and our mats. There was just the hint of a new moon and just enough starlight to see the road.

I walked alone feeling comfortable in my long robe. I was passed by several people before I felt a hand on my shoulder and turned to see Kazz and Takizawa. We walked together for a while before I asked Takizawa the first question that popped into my mind: Why didn't he bring his sword?

Kazz answered for him, "The teacher always carries the mental body of a sword. It's not important for him to have the actual sword."

Then I asked if Takizawa had experienced another vision, perhaps like the one two years earlier in Osaka of the Kremlin collapsing.

"For many years, at the fire ceremony," the teacher answered, "I felt God falling down into the fire. Always God goes into the fire. But not this time. This time God stayed in the high place and tossed ashes from the sky into the fire. The fire pushed the ashes back into the air where they dropped again on the fire. The fire pushed the ashes back. This happened three times. The last time the gods stayed in the ashes and went all over the world, covering all the bad and evil spirits. It will be difficult for war to start now, with the earth covered in ashes."

"Because of the project?" I asked. "Because of the stone gods?"

"Yes," he answered. "However…" We passed a group of silent participants. When they saw the teacher they stopped and bowed reverently.

"There is a problem," the teacher finally said after we continued down the hill. "We are missing two important places.

"We need gods in South Africa and the Amazon."

It was Kazz who asked, "Do you know anyone going there? I can't."

"Not me," I said. "I'm finished traveling for a while."

"No problem," said Kazz quickly. "We'll find a way."

Then I heard myself say, "Oh, don't worry. I'll take care of it."

Back in Tokyo, several days after the fire ceremony, I lay in a tub at my hotel. My body ached from a sudden flu, and I couldn't move. The mineral salts relaxed my muscles but I was overheated. "What have I done?" I thought. "Why have I accepted more gods? I don't have the power yet. I've stretched way too far, too fast." I pulled the plug and watched the water slip over my chest and legs on its way down the drain. Drifting into a delirium, I saw myself flowing into the drain along with the water. I saw a windmill, the blades spinning round and round until they turned into a waterfall cascading into the tub. Then the bow of a ship appeared. A Viking ship? The vessel became a funeral pyre, drifting aflame. Was it *my* funeral I was witnessing? The ship changed into a myriad of shapes and forms. Then there was a huge storm. A hand from the burning ship reached into the swirling water and grabbed me just before I sank through the drain.

I slowly pulled myself out of the tub. Then I lay on my bed, mentally kicking myself. South Africa? The Amazon? What the hell was I thinking?

chapter 20

At the Cape of Good Hope in South Africa.

Walls

Man is
a great wall builder
The Berlin Wall
The Wailing Wall of Jerusalem
But the wall
most impregnable
Has a moat
flowing with fright
around his heart

A wall without windows
for the spirit to breeze through

A wall
without a door
for love to walk in

—Oswald Mtshali, South African poet

The gods hit my cold bedroom floor like tombstones. Kazz had given me three gods, one for South Africa, one for the Amazon, and one to place anywhere in either Africa or South America. I dropped the rest of my luggage, which smelled of jet fuel, nearby. No one was waiting for me this time. Juan Li was off doing his Tai Chi. There was a terse letter from Donna. "Please don't write or call. It's too painful for me."

The years of working on the Sword of Heaven stretched out into eternity. "I'll be dead from old age before this project is finished," I thought. South Africa and the Amazon are so far away. Maybe I could do one trip in the winter, another in the spring. South Africa wouldn't be easy with all the trouble there. But again, nothing had been easy. Why should this be any different?

For the next month, as the winter holidays approached, I felt as if the stone gods were tied to my arms and legs. I went dully through my assignments taking uninspired pictures, wondering if the power I had felt in New York and Japan would return.

Yet unlike the winter that Donna and I returned from Japan, the world was a friendly place: there were no car accidents, no death threats, illness. Instead the phone rang constantly with prospects for work, and unlikely people offered words of encouragement.

At a Christmas party I ran into Don George, the editor who had published my first Shinto article several years before. He was now the *San Francisco Examiner's* travel editor,

and suggested that I call Varig, the Brazilian airline. "Use my
name. Tell them you're writing a travel story." George couldn't
help with South Africa, which was an off-limits story to most
travel publications because of the international boycott.

Then one day my landlord, Doug DeVries, stopped by. I
told him about my dilemma, the problem of organizing two
major sojourns below the equator. He suggested doing both
at once. "Have you ever looked at a map to see how close
Rio de Janeiro is to South Africa?"

As my plans shaped up, I wrote Kazz to tell him the good
news. I would travel by Varig to Rio, then catch a flight to
Johannesburg. I would first place a god in South Africa, then
on my way back, I would place two gods in South America.
Varig discounted me a three-week, unlimited plane pass so I
could fly to the Amazon as well as to Iguaçu Falls, where
Paraguay, Argentina, and Brazil meet. My landlord had told
me that Iguaçu rivaled Niagara in both size and beauty. It
sounded like a perfect place for the third god.

Kazz wrote back saying to be especially careful, that the
teacher had warned him that South Africa and the Amazon
were powerful places. He reminded me of the special chants
I had learned at Iwakiyama and not to forget to take the
replica of the sword with me. He wished me good luck, and
said that the group would conduct a special ceremony to
protect me.

The trip began on the 28th of February, 1988, the first day
of the Chinese New Year. It was the Year of the Dragon, the

same legendary animal under which both Kazz and I were born. In my growing excitement about the trip, I imagined a dramatic ending to the project: I would be arrested as a danger to the state by a South African goon squad:

"No, no, don't take him away," a voice would cry from a crowd that had gathered to give me a hero's welcome. "He was only doing it for our good. For the world. Don't punish him!"

Finally, after a worldwide outcry I would be released. "No, not the Nobel Peace Prize!" I'd say humbly. "I really don't deserve it. But my Japanese teacher, it was his idea."

Or maybe I'd be captured by a wild Amazon tribe. I would impress them with a few tricks I had learned from the teacher, and they would revere me as their wizard. Then I would be found by a group of California ecologists who happened to be on a safari to protect the rain forests or something.

Or, a romantic ending: I'd meet a beautiful woman who'd think that placing Shinto gods was heroic, that I was a brave warrior fighting for peace. She wouldn't question my motives. She wouldn't argue with me. She would support me (and she would be rich, of course). I wasn't clear what would happen after I met her, and we fell in love. Maybe the ending should take place at an airport, like the final scene in *Casablanca*. A kiss and goodbye? Hello? Should I go or should I stay?

It was all good fantasy. In real life, the closure I craved would come—but not as I fantasized.

For a few moments, at the Johannesburg airport, I thought one of my fantasies had materialized. She was standing alone, reading a map. She had long dark hair, pulled gracefully back, and she was wearing red-framed glasses. Even with travel-worn clothes she looked urbane and sophisticated. When the downtown bus pulled up she got on first, so I followed and sat next to her. She was French but spoke good English. We had been on the same plane from Rio, it turned out. I asked if I might look at her guidebook. I told her it was impossible to find a guidebook on South Africa in the States.

Her name was Pascale and—so much for the romantic fantasy—she was married. She was a medical doctor, from Paris, but lived with her husband, a surgeon, and their child in Tahiti. They were tired of Tahiti, but didn't want to move back to France.

"In France, we are stuck. If we want to switch fields in medicine, even if we go back to school, we are not allowed. If we moved here, we could."

"But why South Africa?" I asked incredulously. "This country is a mess."

"You can't believe everything you read," answered Pascale. "I want to see for myself."

At dinner that night we learned that our itineraries were nearly identical. We agreed to share the cost and driving of a rental car and explore the country together.

Over the next three weeks, we drove more than 3,000

miles, possible largely because of good roads and Pascale's passion for fast driving. We started in Johannesburg and crossed the Transvaal to Krueger National Park, then through the independent country of Swaziland and along the Indian Ocean coast past Durban and Port Elizabeth before ending our travels in Cape Town.

I saw incredible wealth, clean modern cities, and the most developed highway system in all of Africa. It was not only human wealth: the countryside burst with fertility and possibility.

And yet I always reminded myself that we traveled the white man's road, a privileged road which led mostly to white homes and farms. We saw the other roads from a distance. They were small, narrow, full of potholes. These were the roads that led to the other South Africa, to the townships and to the homelands. I only knew about these areas from books, magazines, and film. I would have liked to explore and attempt to understand that part of South Africa, but it would have to wait for another trip.

Pascale and I traveled well together, and I appreciated her insight and companionship. But when we discussed politics, we invariably argued.

I'd recite my book knowledge and point out the huge inequities that existed between the whites who, with 18 percent of the population, had confined the blacks to 13 percent of the land. She replied that the rest of Africa lived in dismal poverty and disease.

"You are so critical of the whites," Pascale would say. "Give them a chance! At least they haven't done what your country did to the Indians."

We argued about the international boycott. I said it was necessary to force South Africa into realizing the immorality of the apartheid system, and she argued that putting the economy into a tailspin mostly hurt the poor, a position backed up by nearly all the nonwhites we spoke with.

"You Americans are so self-righteous, so quick to judge. What do you know about this country?"

She had a point. I was finding South Africa as difficult to understand as Japan. During our stay in Johannesburg, we met a man named Adrian Turgel, a white man in his early 30s. Adrian spoke nearly perfect Zulu, and had been arrested several times for his advocacy of black property rights. He immediately corrected me when I called the situation in South Africa a problem between blacks and whites.

"No, no," he said impatiently. "It is about tribalism."

He said that among blacks, there were the Zulu-speaking tribes, the Xhosa-speaking tribes, the Tswana-speaking tribes, and the Swazi-speaking tribes—to name just a few—who often feuded with each other. Even within the European community, there were tribal differences: The people of English descent touted distinctly different political and cultural views from the Afrikaners, the South Africans of Dutch descent. The Afrikaners owned and tilled the land. The

English were the traders, the coastal people who favored more liberal policies toward blacks.

But I didn't need books or history lessons to tell me about the prevalence of fear. The fear wasn't only among the blacks and "colored" who daily faced oppression and violence, but also among the fortified and privileged white communities. It hung over the country like a dense smog, inescapable. One day I went to an Afrikaner bank to cash a traveler's check, and before I opened my bag or mouth the teller addressed me in English.

"Why?" I asked.

"You look so relaxed, you have to be a foreigner," she answered.

At one point we were driving through a township near Durban when suddenly, as we turned a corner, we encountered a huge, yellow tank full of soldiers, a "Yellow People Eater," as they were not-so-fondly called.

Another time we picked up a black hitchhiker who told us she worked as a common clerk despite her college degree. "I'm actually colored," she told us, "but why should people ask me whether I'm Indian or black or whatever? I'm HUMAN!"

"Poor South Africa," I said to Pascale after we dropped the woman off. "We can safely drink the water. Big deal."

"If you die from bad water it's a big deal," she said.

After we had been traveling together a while, just after Krueger Park, I told Pascale about the Shinto project. Telling stories is like giving away something precious, and I hoped that she'd appreciate what I was giving her. Instead she listened without comment, and her indifference made my words seem empty. "She thinks I'm a crazy Californian," I thought. "I better shut up."

But later, when I brought up my love life, I realized that she had been listening. I told her about Donna, about our difficulties, and about our eventual split, which I thought was partially caused by my commitment to the Shinto project.

"You chose this project—putting simple stones around the world—over her?" she asked incredulously. "This is what you think? There was something else, no? She was ugly? Stupid? You didn't like her?"

"It's more complicated than that. She wanted to live in New York."

"That doesn't matter. You can make things work if you want," Pascale said quickly. "Didn't she help you?"

"Yes," I said reluctantly. "She was very helpful."

"Did she believe this, this peace project would actually work?"

"I'm not sure. I know she saw it as a kind of huge art project, a performance piece."

"She knew you had to do it alone, right?"

"Well, yes, actually she did say that she understood that it was my project. That's why she didn't want to interfere."

"The hero. I know men like you. They are out to save the

world. You think you have to do this, to prove yourself. I wouldn't have been so patient."

"She wasn't all that patient."

"Do you really think being a hero makes that much difference to a woman?"

"You don't understand."

"Yes, I don't understand," she said. "But you don't either. You haven't figured out where Donna—or any woman— belongs in your life."

"Maybe. But this story isn't about Donna and me."

"Of course it is. All stories are about love. What else is there?"

"Now you sound like her! But how can I talk about women, or even have a relationship, when I haven't even gotten over my own fears?"

I was quiet a long time. I finally said, "Donna and I were like brother and sister. She helped me express my internal world through art. She polished me. I think I helped her too: I helped her to New York where I'm sure she'll be dis-covered. She'll be a famous artist some day, I know it.

"We were good for each other, really," I said. "But I think we pushed it about as far as we could. I wasn't ready to be with a woman in another way."

"Then maybe that should be your next project," she said. "Women. It would be more interesting and you might learn something really useful."

After nearly three weeks in South Africa, I still carried the Shinto god. It wasn't for lack of choice: there was the fantastic beauty of the Transvaal and Krueger Park, and the dramatic Indian Ocean coast. Of course, I could always point to some tangible reason for not placing the god: lack of water, simple privacy, or convenience. But mostly I just felt not now. Relax. Have faith.

By the time we arrived in Durban, on the southern coast, I was tired and irritable. It didn't help when I saw a white woman yank her three-year-old from a freshwater pool at a playground near the beach. The child was playing with two black children her age, and the mother had a fit. The child reached sadly back to her playmates. It was a pitiful sight, worse even than the signs on the beach designating "whites only" areas. "Why the hell can't they get it together," I thought. "Stupid people! They have so much, why don't they just share?" Pascale, who witnessed the scene, was also shocked.

The next day, at a hotel restaurant in Port Elizabeth, we met a South African doctor and his wife, who was from Namibia. He was an expatriate now, living in Canada, who had just returned to South Africa for a short vacation. I told him about the incident. He looked embarrassed and shrugged.

He told us that he had left his native country for three

reasons: he didn't want to serve in the army; he could make more money in Canada; and apartheid. In that order.

"South Africa will have black rule eventually," he said. "It's inevitable. But it will take an act of God, a miracle, divine intervention to make it a peaceful transition."

Pascale listened to him carefully. Like me, she hadn't found what she was looking for. The bland towns bored her. The food was uninspired. She was getting fed up with the people. How could she live and work in this environment? What would she tell her husband?

"Isn't there any place in South Africa one can get a decent meal? Go to a concert? An opera?" she asked.

"You haven't been to Cape Town?" the doctor asked.

I said no, it was our last destination. We'd probably be there tomorrow.

"It's different," he said, "You'll see."

We returned to our separate rooms. A refrigerator motor kicked in and I turned on the television to drown out the noise. *Dallas,* the American soap, was playing, and I turned the TV off. I stuffed plugs into my ears. Before I fell into an anxious sleep, I wondered what I would do if Cape Town wasn't right. Where would I place the god? I couldn't stay in South Africa forever.

When the nightmare began, I was at the top of the stairs leading out of the bomb shelter, rather than inside. The violent noise, which usually came from behind the escape hatch, now came from behind the door, which I slammed shut after running up the stairs. I was terrified as usual. But this time I looked around me and saw Kazz and the teacher dressed in white robes. As they waved swords above their heads, they chanted.

I turned back to the door and cried the words, Amaterasu-Omikami, repeating the name of the Sun Goddess over and over. I reached for the doorknob. Suddenly the door flung open. An evil stench slammed into me. Then something horrible, without form, gripped me. I struggled and turned back to Kazz and the teacher, but they had disappeared. I was alone.

"Go away! Go away!" I screamed. Never had I confronted the creature who guarded the door. I felt nauseated and overwhelmed. The more I struggled, the more I became entwined with the creature. I reached for the doorknob and grabbed it for support.

I don't know where the voices came from. They were soft and tender and not at all filled with terror. I was suddenly aware of my heart beating furiously. For the first time since Kazz and the teacher disappeared, I felt the presence of others—powerful others, who, like the evil one, were formless. I had the vague feeling that these were the spirits of the great teachers of the world: Buddha, Mohammed, Confucius, and Christ. They were all talking to me. Then it was only Christ's voice I heard.

"You!" I cried.

"Who did you expect?" the voice answered calmly.

"Help me!"

"Let go. Relax. Open your heart."

I began to pray. It was a very simple prayer. It wasn't for me; it was for the people of South Africa, so full of fear and hate.

Then I took a deep breath, and as I released the air I imagined myself pliant like a willow tree. All the while the evil swept past me in spasms, buffeting me with unimaginable force. This went on for a long time, but I kept breathing deeper and deeper, imagining that my heart was opening wider and wider until it encompassed the very evil itself. Then I let go of my grip on the doorknob, and suddenly I was on the other side feeling porous and floating happily above the stairs. There was no sign of the beast or the door.

When I awoke, I was clutching the tiny sword Kazz had given me for protection. I turned to my side and placed it carefully on the dresser. I had found my power. I rolled over and fell back into an easy sleep.

The next morning I was relieved when Pascale offered to
drive. I pushed my seat back, so exhausted from my night of
revelation that I hardly noticed the fantastic speeds she was
hitting. I stared at the green hills, then at the well-tended
vineyards that bordered the road. Far away, lightning struck a
mountain range. Huge bolts shattered the air, and I watched
the show with amazement. The world was so beautiful, and
I felt at peace.

After a while, I dozed.

"Cape Town!" Pascal cried, slapping my leg. "It's beautiful."

The sky cleared, except for one small cloud which
spouted a rainbow that dropped to a cluster of elegant
buildings. Pascale stopped the car so I could snap a picture.
Table Mountain rose abruptly 3,500 feet above the town, its
sheer cliffs wet from the rain. Wisps of fog swirled around
the summit.

As we drove to the center we both felt an immediate
change. This town was unlike anything we had seen in the
rest of South Africa. If Johannesburg felt like Los Angeles,
with its impersonal high-rises and suburbs sprawling out
from no apparent center, Cape Town was like San Francisco.
The streets were crooked and narrow, the buildings old,
dating all the way back to 1652 when the city was founded

by Dutch traders. The air was sweet and fresh from the two oceans that met at the Cape. I felt at home.

We found a lovely old hotel near the spacious legislative complex. The clerk was friendly and relaxed. That night we dined on ostrich steaks and fresh salad, and agreed it was the best food we'd eaten in South Africa. As we strolled the city after dinner we saw people of different races walking hand in hand. I went to sleep confident that I had found a place for the god.

I envisioned that when the time came for me to place the god, I would go alone. I couldn't imagine Pascale would be interested. But when I told her my plans, she wanted to come along.

"At first, I was sure you didn't know what you were doing," she said. "But you are so persistent."

"You thought it was stupid."

"It might be. It might not. Now I'm not sure."

Together we drove along the north shore of the Cape. We stopped at a supermarket that could have been transplanted from the United States and bought a roasted chicken, bread and wine. We picnicked on a huge boulder overlooking the Atlantic Ocean, watching seals play carelessly in the combers. Near the car a baboon arrogantly strolled in search of a tourist handout. We gave it a banana and drove on.

At the Cape of Good Hope, there were hordes of German and British tourists posing on the ledge overlooking the Indian and Atlantic oceans. It was foggy with intermittent blue.

I found a ledge about 150 meters above the water and watched the two seas join together between puffs of wind and fog. Pascale placed herself on a ledge above me and snapped pictures as I steadied myself in preparation for throwing the god.

"Careful," she yelled down at me. "Don't get so close to the ledge."

There was no need for worry. I wasn't going to slip or jump. There would be no such dramatic ending to this story. The finale had already occurred. It was that moment in my nightmare when I finally had the power to face my worst fears and open the escape hatch door. It was the spirits, who I'd finally accepted, that helped me approach and open the door, but it was the receptiveness of my heart—love—which had ultimately protected and saved me from the evil.

And what did I find on the other side of the door? I found a world where fear wasn't in control. A world where I could allow the good around me in. Without fear to stop me, I felt I could finally engage in life in a way that I never knew possible before.

The god left my hand and flew through the air. It splashed, just off the rocky beach, into the crashing surf.

Pascale waved and said we should leave soon. She was flying back to Johannesburg in a few hours, while I had a return ticket to Brazil where I would place my last two Shinto gods. I stared across the two oceans for a long time before scrambling up the cliff.

After South Africa I returned to Rio de Janeiro. There I retrieved the two gods I had left earlier for safekeeping with the manager of a hotel on the *praia* Copacabana. I then took a short plane ride to the international airport at Iguaçu Falls, on the borders of Brazil, Paraguay, and Argentina. At the falls, under helicopters carrying gawking tourists, I threw one of the gods into a deep, turbulent part of the river. The spot was framed by a rainbow created by the cascading torrent of water and the bright noon sun.

I flew back to Rio and caught a plane to Manaus, the wild frontier town situated in the heart of the Amazon jungle. By now I was sick and exhausted from a grueling six weeks. I boarded the *Marreiro II* and placed the final god at the point where the Rio Negro and the Rio Solimoes meet and become the Amazon. It seemed a fitting spot to end my involvement with the Sword of Heaven. Two waters, as distinctly different as Kazz and me, meet to form one great body of water moving toward the sea.

EPILOGUE

High mountains
are worn down by the waters,
and the valleys
are filled up.

epilogue

San Francisco, April 1999

I've spent the last eleven years slowly readying this story for print, this time with both Kazz's and the teacher's encouragement. I'm back in San Francisco after living two years in Prague and four years in Washington, D.C. From my North Beach window, I can nearly see the apartment where I first heard of the Sword of Heaven in 1982, seventeen years ago. I can see the Golden Gate Bridge and beyond to the Pacific Ocean where Kazz and Juan placed a god together. I've twisted around the spine of a spiral, and although it looks like I'm back where I started, I'm not. The world has changed and so have I.

Many times as I set down this story, I struggled with pen to paper. As Donna so wisely observed, it's hard for me to say how I feel, to articulate what I want, and to fully reveal myself. I even considered telling the story instead with a simple haiku poem accompanied by a photograph:

The gods, placed
oh!
Green parrots in the trees

But I was ultimately compelled to tell the story completely and faithfully, in much the same way I was compelled to help place Shinto gods around the world. The writing, like the project itself, became an act of personal exploration, an act of reflection and growth. It was—as so aptly represented by the cross that Kazz gave me at the monastery—an act of becoming, not being.

Remarkable events have continued to occur since I placed the last gods in South Africa and South America: on November 9, 1989, the Berlin Wall fell. Václav Havel was elected president of a democratic Czechoslovakia on December 29, 1989. Shortly after that, the USSR and the Warsaw Pact ceased to exist. Then, miraculously, apartheid was dismantled in South Africa in 1991, peacefully. The Cold War is over. The fear of an all-out nuclear war between the superpowers is virtually gone.

Did a Shinto priest save the world?

At moments, when I'm switched to the Shinto channel, I think he did. I can clearly see gods all over the world battling in unison for world peace, making sure a missile isn't launched here, helping tear a wall down there. But then, my rational mind, strong as ever, changes the channel, and I think all of it was just a lucky coincidence.

I can say unequivocally, however, that a Shinto priest changed *my* life. My crippling nightmare has never returned. With fear removed from my heart, I've lived a very different life.

In 1992, while I was in Prague waiting to meet my old friend Wolfgang, I met Rebecca Taggart, a foreign service officer at the U.S. Embassy. After just a few days together, I decided that she was the woman I wanted to spend the rest of my life with. But I still lived in San Francisco, and she lived in Prague. It took everything I learned from the Sword of Heaven to make the relationship work. I jumped in with both feet, and after returning to San Francisco for six weeks to put my business in order and to pack up my things, I returned to Prague. There were moments when I doubted my rash decision, but I've learned that doubts are a normal part of life. There were times when our romance was less than perfect, but I've learned to live with that too.

After two years in Prague—where we both witnessed and participated in the country's thrilling transition to a free, democratic state—we moved to Washington, D.C. Then, a year later, at an outdoor ceremony in Northern California, surrounded by a grove of redwood trees, we were married. Kazz flew in from Japan to officiate and make sure no bad spirits interfered. Two years later, our daughter Miranda Kristina was born. Kazz wrote to congratulate us and referred to her as the daughter of the Sword of Heaven.

I haven't been back to Japan since the fire ceremony, but I know from Kazz that the teacher Hakuryu Takizawa is still alive, although suffering from Alzheimer's disease. Kazz doesn't think he will live much longer. My teacher—and I say "my" purposefully—is more than 90 years old, and I thank him from deep inside my heart for all he has done. I wish his soul a well-earned rest.

About ten years ago, Kazz told me he had finished the project by placing two final gods—one in a pyramid near Mexico City, helped by Juan Li, and one in North Korea along with the teacher and a group of the teacher's disciples. But I wouldn't be surprised that if the world suddenly got really dangerous, a package would appear on my doorsteps with a note, "One Shinto God."

Juan Li has become a renowned Tai Chi teacher. Donna still lives and works as an artist in New York. We are still in touch and recently she shared some of her memories of our time together to help me tell this story. Pascale is back in France with her husband and their four children.

As I write these last words, rays from the afternoon sun are striking my office window. The golden light is wonderful. I love this city, and I am so happy to be back. I can hear my daughter and her friend talking in the room next to me. I think about their future. The Cold War is over, and so is the nuclear threat of my childhood. My daughter won't grow up in a bomb shelter but that doesn't mean the world is not dangerous.

I want to tell my daughter not to be afraid, but I know that she will have her own fears and her own unique solutions. Instead, I'll tell her to be vigilant, and to look to her dreams and nightmares for clues and signs of progress. I'll tell her to be open-minded about the spirit world, and if it feels right, to call upon the spirits for help. I'll also tell her to seek out communities embarked on meaningful and noble acts. The acts need not be as large as the Sword of Heaven, for any act that makes the world a better place is worthy. Above all, I'll tell her that all action, big or small, must always be accompanied by the opening of one's heart. As the Sword of Heaven taught me, ritual only takes one to the door. To get through to the other side, there must be love.

The afternoon light moves from the end of my desk and for a moment illuminates the letters on my keyboard. From my window, I can see a huge ship passing beneath the Golden Gate Bridge on its way to dock. I lean back and take it all in. I wonder where the ship is going next. I wonder where the light will fall now.

Mikkel Aaland

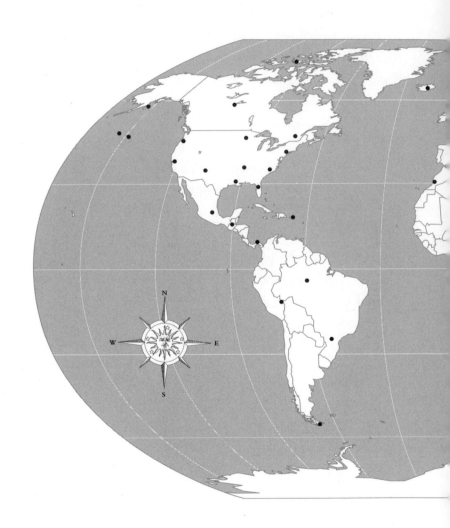

sword of heaven placement information

Compiled by Kazz Tagami

1. North of Spitbergen, Norway
2. Antarctica
3. Lake Titicaca, Peru
4. Cape Horn, Chile
5. New York, USA
6. San Francisco, California, USA
7. Upper Mississippi River, USA
8. Hawaii, USA
9. Sun & Moon Lake, Taiwan
10. Hong Kong
11. Macao
12. Bangkok, Thailand
13. Calcutta, India
14. Nepal
15. Nepal
16. Darjeeling, India
17. Peking, China
18. Harbin, China
19. North of Manchuria, China
20. Nachodka, USSR
21. Lake Baikal, USSR
22. Moscow, USSR
23. Black Sea, USSR
24. Athens, Greece
25. Brienzer Lake, Switzerland
26. London, England
27. Paris, France
28. Florence, Italy
29. North Cape, Norway
30. Tromso, Norway
31. Bear Island, Norway
32. Lake Inari, Finland
33. Helsinki, Finland
34. Copenhagen, Denmark
35. Geiranger Fjord, Norway
36. Northwestern Norway
37. Panama Canal, Panama
38. Tipasa Beach, Algeria
39. Montreal, Canada
40. Athabasca River, Alberta, Canada
41. Azorou, Morroco
42. Ulefoss, Norway
43. Tibet near Lasa, China
44. Western China
45. Colombo, Sri Lanka

46. Male, Maldive Islands
47. Madras, India
48. Louisiana, USA
49. Cheju Island, Korea
50. New Caledonia
51. Madurai, India
52. Himachal Pradesh, India
53. Northern India
54. Northern India
55. Mount Kangchenjunga, India
56. Lake Naivasha, Kenya
57. Sea of Galilee, Israel
58. Minnesota, USA
59. Washington, USA
60. North Carolina, USA
61. New Mexico USA
62. Kachemak Bay, Alaska, USA
63. Eastern China
64. Eastern China
65. Eastern China
66. Eastern China
67. Eastern China
68. Xi'an, China
69. Florida, USA
70. Nile River, Egypt
71. Zamboanga City, Philippines
72. Singapore
73. Kun Lung Mountains, China
74. Northern Pakistan
75. Lake Lögurinn, Iceland
76. Karachi, Pakistan
77. Islamabad, Pakistan
78. Bombay, India
79. Mount Kailas, Tibet
80. Tibet
81. Berlin, Germany
82. Baltic Sea, Sweden
83. Midway Islands
84. Perth, Australia
85. Melbourne, Australia
86. Vieques, Puerto Rico
87. Cyprus
88. Mount Massada, Israel
89. Tel Aviv, Israel
90. Dead Sea, Israel
91. Jerusalem, Israel
92. Suez Canal, Egypt
93. Mount Sinai, Egypt
94. Gulf of Arabia
95. Aman, Jordan
96. Mount Ararat, Turkey
97. Persian Gulf, Iran
98. Mashhad, Iran
99. Teheran, Iran
100. Elazig, Turkey
101. Lake Atítlan, Guatemala
102. Mexico City, Mexico
103. Cape of Good Hope, South Africa
104. Iguaçu Falls, Brazil
105. Manaus, Brazil
106. Near Magnetic Pole, Canada
107. Loch Ness, Scotland
108. Bali

acknowledgements

This project spans seventeen years and I have accumulated a debt of gratitude to a large community of people who helped me along the way. Besides the people noted in the narrative, I'd like to thank Melinda Tevis, whose dinner party in 1982 and friendship started the whole thing. Thanks to Michael Rogers and Anne Russell who patiently read most every draft of the story. Thanks to Tom Mogensen, Dave Drum, Jacques Gauchey, Michelle Vignes, Monica Suder, Michaela Schreier, and Perry Garfinkel, dear friends who gave their valuable advice and encouragement from the beginning of the project to the end.

Thanks to my friends who came to the project at later stages but offered just as much enthusiasm and support: Jo Ellen "the whip" Bokar, Janelle Balnicky, Kate Kelly, Michael Borek, Rudy Burger, Laena Wilder, Paul Saffo, Laura Parker, Chris Vail, Jan Hopson, James Houston, Michael Lester, Mark Powelson, Daniel Ben-Horin, Valerie Russell, Suzanne Lavoie, and Eva Patterson. Special thanks to Bernard Ohanian for his long hours with the manuscript and patience with me on the courts.

Thanks to Lucy McCauley for reading and carefully critiquing the manuscript and for putting me in touch with the receptive folks at Travelers' Tales.

Thanks to Sarah Lazin, as usual, for her wise legal and creative consul.

Thanks also to other friends, family, and colleagues who encouraged or advised me at various stages of the project: Rebecca Abrams, Nathan Benn, Hal Hinson, Laura Levy, Sarah Margulies, Sean Parker, Bob Wilkinson, Beverly Usher, Seth Derish, Dawn Finch, Maggie Hallahan, Jerry Mander, Sandy Close, Karen Robbins, Wendy Vetter, Chuck McIntyre, Valerie Robbins, Jack Swanson, Steve Moni, Leonard Koren, Mirek Vodrazka, Amy Shiffman, Ellen McNeilly, Paul Persons, Marcia Briggs, Laura Oliver, Elizabeth Logan Harris, Julie Westcott, Dorit Elder, Francisca Schneider, Catherin Fredman, Fred Soloway, Catherine Henderson, Marsha Weiner, Paul Foldes, Saucy Dollard, Dayna Macy, Jennifer Saffo, Rob Fulop, Vanessa Southern, Michael Taggart, Annette Doornbus, Noel Young, Robert Stricker, Michael Larson, Miyako Yoneyama, Sally Larsen, Charles Wehrenberg, Barbara Bode, Dana Hull, Laura Nolan, Peter Goodman, Jeff Hunter, Gregg Mitchell, Richard Koman, Catherine Fowler, Joe Kane, and my family on both sides of the Atlantic.

I'd especially like to thank the people at Travelers' Tales who took a rough stone and polished it into a thing of beauty: Lisa Bach, Larry Habegger, Sean O'Reilly, James O'Reilly, Tim O'Reilly, and designer Diana Howard.

Finally, I want to acknowledge the emotional and editorial support of my wife, Rebecca Taggart. I wouldn't have finished this book without her help.

"Bert the Turtle" excerpted from *Life Under a Cloud* by Allan M. Winkler, published by Oxford University Press, 1993.

Selection from *Children of Hiroshima*, published by Taylor & Francis Ltd., London, 1980.

Selection from "Eve of Destruction," Words and Music by P. F. Sloan. Copyright © 1965 by Duchess Music Corporation. MCA Music Publishing, a Division of Universal Studios, Inc. International Copyright Secured. All Rights Reserved.

Selection from *Freedom from Fear and Other Writings* by Aung San Suu Kyi, published by Penguin Books, 1991.

Selections from the *I Ching*, The Richard Wilhelm Translation, published by Princeton University Press, 1978.

Walls by Oswald Mtshali. All rights reserved.

Author's note: You can find an updated bibliography of Shinto books and resources as well as color and additional *sumi-e* photographs at my web site http://www.cyberbohemia.com/Pages/Sword.htm.

About the photographs on the four part-opener pages: To help illustrate the book I created a style of photography that I call *sumi-e* photography, which was inspired by the Japanese art of gestural painting. Instead of using a brush and black ink, I waved or shook a 35 mm camera at slow shutter speeds, mostly in front of boats, stones, trees, and sand, leaving the results largely to chance. The text is from the *I Ching*, the ancient Eastern book of wisdom.